Chi non lavora non mangia – chi lavora mangia!

Who does not work does not eat – who works, eats!

Dedicated to
John P. Raynor, S.J.
President Emeritus
Marquette University
Milwaukee, Wisconsin

Around the Corner
From Shoeshine Boy to College President

By Louis C. Vaccaro, Ph.D.

Edited by Renee Lapham Collins

Copyright © 2011 by Louis C. Vaccaro and Renee Lapham Collins
Book Design and editing by Renee Lapham Collins
Formatting by Megan Pavlak
Cover by Jody Donaghy Woltman
"Bootblacks in and Around City Hall Park, 1920snNY" *Courtesy of the Library of Congress*

ISBN 0-7414-6597-3

Printed in the United States of America

Published June 2011

INFINITY PUBLISHING
1094 New DeHaven Street, Suite 100
West Conshohocken, PA 19428-2713
Toll-free (877) BUY BOOK
Local Phone (610) 941-9999
Fax (610) 941-9959
Info@buybooksontheweb.com
www.buybooksontheweb.com

Contents

Dedication

Words alone are inadequate to express my thanks and appreciation to the many people who have helped me in countless ways in the preparation and actual writing of this life story. If I were to name each and every person who helped shape my life, and eventually recount my life in this book, it would take several additional chapters. I am not a writer by profession. My work over the years includes being a husband, father, teacher, mentor, and, in some measure, an unofficial ambassador for the U.S. in several foreign countries.

I will be the first to confess that I was not outstanding in any of these areas or responsibilities, but I tried to do my best with the gifts God has given me, gifts nurtured by grandparents, parents, teachers, siblings, uncles and aunts, cousins and on and on. Whatever success I was able to achieve was not the result of raw talent but rather the help, inspiration, support and love provided by each of the above.

However, I would be remiss if I did not single out several key persons, mentors and colleagues, notably Fr. John P. Raynor, S.J., Fr. Ted Hesburgh, C.S.C., and Dr. Prudence Bostwick, as well as every grade school and high school teacher and numerous university professors, the names of whom I'm unable to fully remember.

In the actual writing of this life story, I am especially indebted to Renee Lapham Collins, and for the special cover and layout provided by Jodi Donaghy Woltman, both former students at Siena Heights (College) University and both very successful in their chosen professions.

Whatever errors occur in this book are solely my responsibility and if I have offended or slighted anyone, I do apologize and ask for their understanding. In the final analysis, I owe overwhelming gratitude to each person who touched my life in so many ways, especially the love of my life, my wife Linda Lee Vaccaro, and my former wife, Jean Hudak Murray. My children whom I adore, but have rarely expressed my complete and unconditional love deserve more than my gratitude by helping me become more human and whose understanding I pray will increase if they succeed in wading through this book, which is also dedicated to them, my grandparents and Mama and Papa.

Ad majorem dei glorium, "All for the greater glory of God."

Louis C. Vaccaro, Ph.D.
Las Vegas
February 2011

Foreword

W hen I agreed to write the foreword to this book, I was unaware that my long-time friend began his career as a shoeshine boy on the streets of Los Angeles. Although Lou Vaccaro and I first met in 1961, the year he began teaching at St. Mary's College, Notre Dame, details of his childhood in California never came up in our many conversations over the years. Later, when Lou was appointed the first lay vice president at the University of Portland in Oregon, we had many opportunities to meet and chat, but he never mentioned he was once in the shoeshine business.

I was surprised but pleased to read the details of his immigrant family upbringing and subsequent vocation as an academic, primarily in Catholic higher education. Because Lou served as a vice president at the Holy Cross-sponsored University of Portland, we had more than a few conversations about the issues and challenges of operating a Catholic university, especially during the turbulent late 1960s. One of the recurring themes in our intermittent talks was the question of how to determine the identity of a Catholic college or university. He might phone or buttonhole me at a meeting and eventually pose the question,

"How does one build a first-rate Catholic university?" This question, I thought, might reflect his struggle with some related issues of governance, such as questions of authority within a religiously sponsored institution and related matters. One day when the question came up, I replied, "One builds a first-rate Catholic university by first building a first-rate university."

This meant the absolute essentials for any first-rate university begin with attracting the right faculty and bright, promising students.

Lou and I spent even more time discussing how to come up with the money to attract such talent. Lou's career was very different from mine. He served in the U.S. Air Force during the Korean War; he married, raised a large family and criss-crossed the country in pursuit of his post-graduate degrees. Later, he worked with the Holy Cross fathers, Jesuits, Sisters of Saint Joseph and Adrian Dominican Sisters. He also served six years as president of a prestigious Baptist-founded women's college, all the while remaining an active teacher and scholar and developing an extensive, far-reaching international network and affiliations with colleges and universities abroad. In this context, we would sometimes discuss our common love for China and his devotion to the ongoing work of assisting international students in their efforts to study in the U.S. At last count, according to Lou, he has assisted more than 300 Chinese students in coming to the U.S. to begin and complete their studies. Many of these students have returned to China, but the majority

Fr. Ted Hesburgh with JFK at Notre Dame in 1961. Photo courtesy University of Notre Dame archives.

remained in America, some as successful profession-
als in medicine and banking and some as professors
in leading colleges and universities including the
University of California, Princeton and even St. John's
University in New York.

Whenever my friend was encouraged to write his
autobiography, he would counter, "Someday, when I
have the time." Lucky for him, a Siena graduate and
friend, Renee Collins, volunteered to do the job if Lou
supplied the memories. His book, *Around the Corner:
From Shoeshine Boy to College President*, is the result
of their collaboration. Lou's story is filled with a
lifetime of memories and details tracing his humble
beginnings and subsequent journey through a life
devoted to God and family. I think you will find Lou's
story informative, inspirational, and enjoyable.

Theodore M. Hesburgh, C.S.C.
President Emeritus
The University of Notre Dame

Papa, with Virgie, Joseph and Lou.

Chapter 1
Family Influence

M ost people I know usually speak openly about the influence of their parents during their early and formative years. Try as I might, it is nigh impossible for me to limit my early years' influence to only my mother and father—Mama and Papa. Growing up in a large immigrant family, there were many more family members and relatives whose influence was felt throughout my years of growing up in our large home at 1467 Dana Street and later in Tarzana and Van Nuys, California.

It was not only Mama and Papa but also Big Nonno, Little Nonna and scores of uncles, aunts and cousins whose influence in my life was so profound. But, without question, the largest and most influential person who played such a dramatic role in my life was "Papa," my father. His presence in my life was immediate and dramatic and strangely enough, continues to this day. Although he died rather unexpectedly at the young age of 61, his death was not only unexpected—it was a great shock and loss to me in more ways than one.

I can still recall, in vivid detail, the day I received the telephone call from my brother-in-law Ron Kistler the morning of Friday, December 13, 1963. Having just begun my first academic assignment since receiving my final degree from Michigan State University, I was finally settled with my family in Milwaukee at Marquette University earning $9,200 a year (more than three times what we were living on at MSU), working with the Jesuits at one of their premier universities. Life was good.

Then, the totally unexpected news that my father had died in California while delivering papers with my uncle Pat Lynch began a cascade of grief I had never before known or knew how to handle.

Of course, my life also was greatly influenced by my mother, by grandparents and siblings, but nothing to the degree that Papa had during my growing up years in California. In many ways, our relationship was tension-filled and never warm. He was such an overpowering personality, my reaction to him was a combination of fear, respect, admiration and apprehension. Most days, Papa was barking orders, involving me and my siblings in another new project or just making known to me and anyone else within earshot who the boss was. It was Papa and everyone knew it—whether family members, neighborhood kids and even the priests and nuns at St. Agnes School and later St. Elizabeth Parish in Van Nuys. In some ways, Papa ran our family as though he were in charge of a group of military recruits.

I recall, not long after I was stationed at Dow Air Force Base in Bangor, Maine, my commanding officer asking me what branch of the service I had been in prior to enlisting in the USAF in 1951. Major Reginald L. Hayes, a formidable, rather large fighter pilot from Texas, called me to his office to tell me that he was pleased to award me my third stripe because he was impressed with my work ethic and high degree of responsibility in the few months that I had been in his squadron.

"But, Sir," I protested, "I was never in another branch of service—I came into the Air Force directly from my freshman year in junior college."

"Well, hell, Vaccaro," drawled Major Hayes. "That's hard for me to believe!"

He then began to quiz me on my hometown, my family, parents and my home life. As I began describing my early years, dwelling extensively on my father's influence in my life and his demanding authoritarian personality, Major Hayes, who was never one to spare the cuss words he undoubtedly picked up during his formative years in Texas, blurted, "Well, I'll be damned, Vaccaro, sounds to me as though you received your basic training from one tough hombre!"

And looking back on those years, especially the daily work details and projects that Papa meted out without letting up, I guess Major Hayes was 100 percent correct—Papa was indeed one tough hombre. As I have told countless people, family and friends alike, Papa's influence shaped me in ways that I was totally unaware of during those years of demanding work assignments—always tinged with a high degree of tension, respect and fear. The lessons I learned: the value of work, respect, responsibility, fidelity to family and the proper way to approach work and life were drilled into my psyche from my earliest years and remain with me to this day.

Because I did a maximum of listening and observing and a minimum of talking, my verbal skills were lacking. In fact, from day one in kindergarten until I was on my own in the Air Force, I was plagued with a speech impediment—stuttering. It was while in the service, being interviewed for pilots' candidate school that I realized the root cause of my stuttering was the result of my apprehensive and fearful response I had to my father's overpowering personality. Once away from his influence, and following months of self-analysis, I realized I could speak in a normal cadence without stuttering.

My habit of listening and observing served me well in other areas as well. I learned my father was a great storyteller with dozens of humorous and comic stories that he undoubtedly picked up in the East Liberty section of Pittsburgh from his Italian immigrant pals and chums: "Cowboy" DeLuca, "Frankie" Bove, "Kelly" Napilitano and "Sandwich" Palumbo. The East Liberty section in Pittsburgh was 100 percent Italian, sectioned off from the Polish, Irish and Negro sections of the Steel City.

Each year, Papa and Uncle Edward would make 400 gallons of wine—seven barrels of red for the men and one barrel of white for the ladies. The wine often served as a focal point for scores of friends and relatives who would stop by and be entertained by Papa's stories of bygone days. Of course, the Vaccaro children weren't allowed to drink—but we learned quite a bit of Italian folklore and great, hilarious stories of Papa's growing up Italian in Pittsburgh prior to his move to California for health reasons.

Papa, Mama and my sister, Virgie, moved from Pittsburgh to Los Angeles in 1929, mainly on the advice of my father's physician. He was suffering from severe back pain, due primarily to hard physical work as a plumber. While tall and muscular, Papa's health required that he move to a sunnier and healthier locale. And because he could not immediately practice his plumbing trade in California, Papa's first job was driving a taxicab in Los Angeles. Later, he got work as a truck driver with Johnson's Trucking Company and later with the L.A. Times. Later, Papa convinced his sisters, Angeline, Nelly and eventually Jeanette to move to California from Pittsburgh. Papa also persuaded his parents—Big Nonno Giuseppe Vaccaro and Little Nonna Virginia Pergola Vaccaro to sell their modest home in East Liberty and join the growing Vaccaro clan in Los Angeles. This mass migration of family was the basis of my formative years, first on 20th Street and later on Dana Street in Los Angeles.

Papa's motto was *"Chi non lavora non mangia----chi lavora mangia!."* In English, "Who does not work does not eat – Who works, eats!" Thus, we all worked—it was the Italian way and Papa certainly saw to it that we understood the need to work if we were to survive during the Great Depression.

My sister Virgie, short for Virginia, was the eldest, followed by six boys, me, Joseph, Michael, Gerard, Vincent and David. Largely because of Papa's influence and direction, I learned the plumbing trade, how to raise chickens and rabbits and eventually how to start my own businesses, including selling newspapers and shining shoes. In between, I also picked up small jobs washing windows for small business owners, mowing lawns and collecting scrap metal for the war effort. It was just what everyone in our neighborhood did to make ends meet. Most importantly, in Papa's eyes, it kept us out of trouble. His view was if you keep them busy, they will have no time to get into trouble. And so, Major Hayes observation that I received my basic military training at home—from a tough hombre—was certainly true.

Not only did my siblings and I stay out of trouble, we also had little time to do much else other than work, help out at home and study. So, in retrospect, growing up in Los Angeles was a great advantage and kept the seven of us on the straight and narrow—even though we did not realize it at the time.

But I did learn the important lessons in life—hard work, responsibility, respect, honesty and most important, how to obey my parents and all my elders. There was no question that Mama and Papa were proud of their large brood—even though they rarely, if ever, told us—never saying that they loved us, never showing physical affection and rarely demonstrating the kind of hugs and kisses we observed our friends receiving from their parents.

We always knew our parents loved us because they always provided for us. We were clothed, housed, and fed and made to "toe the line." Yes, these were the lessons I learned along the way—some painful, sometimes accompanied by deserving punishment but always applied with good intentions. And Major Hayes was able to see and admire the good results of my growing-up years in the City of Angels with my siblings, uncles, aunts, cousins and, of course, the Dana Street Commandos.

The house on Gilmore St. in Van Nuys where Lou lived with his family from 1943 until Papa died in 1963.

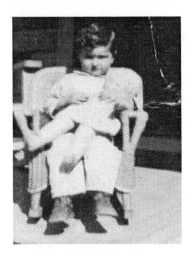

Lou Jr. at 18 months.

Lou Sr. receives an award from the vice president of the Los Angeles Times for his years of service to the company.

The Vaccaro Clan about 1950.

A typical Sunday dinner Italian style in Van Nuys, California, 1950-51.

Chapter 2
The Immigrant Experience

L *ouis C. Vaccaro Jr. was born July 25, 1930 in Los Angeles, the second of seven children of Louis and Louise Vaccaro. He came into the world near the start of the Great Depression, welcomed by parents and grandparents who had traveled to California from southern Italy by way of New York and Pittsburgh, Pennsylvania.*

"Sonny Boy," as his entire family would call him, had a strong work ethic instilled in him almost from the time he was able to understand English and Italian.

My father was the most important person in my life. He provided for us; that's how we knew he loved us. Of course, I loved both my parents and of course my grandparents as well.

My father was a plumber and a truck driver and he saw education as the way to avoid the ranks of the common laborer and would often tell me to stay in school so I did not have to work with my back and my hands.

"Do something where you can use your brain," he would say.

And so I did.

My early life is filled with memories of living the Italian life with its extended family and homemade pasta, bread and wine in the heart of the City of

Angels. Besides my parents, I had five brothers and a sister plus my paternal grandparents and an aunt living in the same house.

My father always had two jobs because there were so many mouths to feed. He would work six and sometimes seven days a week to provide for all of us. I would regularly accompany my father in his plumbing truck as he travelled to various jobs around the city.

My grandparents, Giuseppe and Virginia (Pergola) Vaccaro and Gerardo and Gerarda Vinciguerra all came from the same town in Italy, Potenza, in the province of Basilicata, located in the southernmost part of Italy. Both families immigrated to the U.S. between 1901-1910, coming through Ellis Island. The Vaccaros traveled to California in 1929 while the Vinciguerras stayed in upstate New York.

The elder Vaccaros, in Italian, "Big Nonno" and "Little Nonna," had a great influence on my early life, especially Little Nonna. My grandparents did not have one day of formal schooling. They couldn't read or write, but they were strong, ethical people. My father became a plumber in Pittsburgh and was able to finish vocational high school before he moved to California with my mother and sister. My mother, who grew up in Fredonia/Dunkirk, New York, finished eighth grade before leaving school and going to work to help support the large Vinciguerra family. She worked in a canning factory and later in a factory that produced biscuits and soda crackers. My parents and grandparents had plenty of stories about the "old country," which comprise some of my earliest memories.

My grandmother, Little Nonna, had a tremendous influence on my early life. She was a good listener. She mostly listened since she didn't speak English and I couldn't converse in Italian. In fact, we weren't permitted to speak Italian. Little Nonna taught us card games and many of life's lessons.

When I was going to kindergarten at the Dana Street Elementary School, I was identified as a chronic stutterer and my teacher recommended I work with a speech therapist to overcome my stuttering. So, not only was I shy and fearful of doing something wrong around my father, I was a stutterer. It was hard for me to express myself. Perhaps that's why I was a daydreamer and liked art and music. In fact, I think it was also why I was drawn to singing. I discovered stutterers never stutter when they are singing.

My stuttering stayed with me until I was in the service and away from my father. I'm sure the tension and anxiety of trying to please my father and not saying anything that would make him upset and cause him to yell at me contributed to my stuttering. Once I was away from that influence, stuttering left me.

My grandmother was a great help. She would listen to what I had to say and I never remember stuttering around her. She really cared for my siblings and me.

Lou (right front) was the left tackle for the freshman football team at Los Angeles Valley College in 1950. He is pictured with (from left) Jerry Shutt, Tommie LaVigne, Mike Sutalo, Eddie Taylor and quarterback Tom Poston (in back).

Lou in 1952 in the U.S. Air Force in Bangor, Maine at Dow Air Force Base.

Uncle Joe Vinciguerra immigrated from Italy and later served in the U.S. Army as a cavalryman in World War I. He was gassed and later died from his injuries.

Chapter 3
The Dana Street
Commandos

Dana Street was our haven during the Great Depression.

Growing up in Dana Street neighborhood, we had many advantages. Just one block long, it was within walking distance to Mr. Parker's Malt Shop, the Great American Market, the Dana Street elementary school and playground as well as St. Agnes Catholic Church and School, which housed grades 1-12.

Dana Street was also home to a variety of ethnic groups. Families were Italian, German, Irish, one African American and even a few Latinos. There were only two socio-economic levels among these families: poor middle class and better off middle class, but my friends and I were never aware of which class we occupied.

The corner of Vermont Avenue and Adams Boulevard was central to my life. It was where St. Agnes Church and Catholic School were located, where I sold newspapers—*The Los Angeles Times* and *The Daily News*—and where I began my career as a shoeshine boy.

It also was where the Dana Street Commandos would meet every Saturday and the corner became our home base and our hangout. My brother Joseph, our cousin Bobbie and I formed the Dana Street Commandos in 1941—it was our way to show we were doing our part to fight the Japs and the Nazis. We were joined by neighborhood friends Walter Reardon, Joey Blankmeyer, Art Gillette, and the most notorious of all, Eddie Hamil.

We would frequent the Army surplus store to outfit ourselves with World War II helmet liners, cartridge belts and assorted military insignias. As commandos, we felt a special camaraderie with each other. Those of us still around today continue to refer to ourselves as commandos.

In those days, Eddie was the only one of the gang who did not attend St. Agnes School. Because he came from a strong Southern Protestant family, Eddie always attended the public schools. He also was a couple of years older than we were so we considered him an original tough guy. Eddie used to regale us with stories of his experiences at Foshay Junior High School. Things were so tough at FJHS, which at that time was heavily populated by minority students, Eddie frequently packed a pistol in his waistband.

Eddie also introduced us to the somewhat misdirected adventure of swiping candy and snacks from the Great American Market. It was solely the result of good luck and probably the prayers of my mother and grandmother that kept us from ever being arrested or caught. It was at this same Great American Market that the commandos had one of our most unforgettable adventures with Eddie Hamil.

Great American Fracas

Eddie's mission that day was to introduce us to the basic, easy and highly dangerous maneuver of stealing all the candy we could ever want from the market. As Eddie said, "They have more than they need and we don't have the money to buy any." Hamil logic at its finest!

On that particular Saturday—it was always a Saturday—since that was our day to hang out and do something different—we ambled through the candy and snack section of the market. I watched closely and with something akin to fascination how easily Eddie began filling his pockets while the other guys went on ahead. As Eddie and I approached the end of a long aisle, he turned to me and said, "Where did those shitheads go?"

Eddie rarely called us by name, preferring instead to identify us as "shitheads, farts" or something far worse. Let it be known that Eddie was not only two to three years older than the rest of us, he also was the toughest, bravest and, I might add, smallest of the group. (We thought it had something to do with the fact that he was from the south and the only non-Catholic among us). Because I was the least likely one to challenge or talk back to Eddie, I answered his query with an honest and straightforward reply, matching my words as closely as possible to Eddie's without using "bad" words.

"I think they went to the can," I said, using the less than polite euphemism for "restroom."

"Well, holy crap," barked Eddie. "Let's go get'em."

Eddie and I made our way to the back of the enormous market and climbed the stairs to the second floor. As we approached the door to the men's room, we could hear three of the Commandos' voices and two other voices we didn't recognize.

"Get in there and tell 'em we gotta go!" Eddie ordered.

Not being one to ignore or disobey Eddie, I strode into the "can," where someone immediately grabbed me by the T-shirt.

"Okay, punk, up against the wall and empty your pockets."

I recognized the voice as one of the two unknown people Eddie and I had heard outside the men's room door. His partner was brandishing a pocketknife with a very sharp-looking blade at least six inches long.

All this time, Eddie was outside in the hall waiting for his minions to join him so we could continue on our Saturday adventure. As it turned out, he was waiting and listening. Having heard the conversation, Eddie burst through the door. The same guy that grabbed me attempted to grab Eddie but he wasn't quick enough. As he reached for Eddie, Eddie dropped him with one quick punch to the nose. Immediately, there was blood all over the place. Then, Eddie did what he did best—he used his steel-tipped boots to kick the knife out of the other guy's hand, all the while showering both of them with a barrage of invectives that even we had not previously known existed.

The combination of Eddie's punch to the nose, his deft kick and shower of invectives made short work of the two—all while the other four commandos stood at the sidelines and cheered him on.

"Get 'em, Eddie! Hit 'em, Eddie! Attaboy, Eddie!"

We all began chasing the other guys out the door and down the stairs, yelling "Get outta here, you jerks, call the police, attaboy, Eddie!"

I often wonder whatever happened to Eddie Hamil. In fact, I occasionally get together with some of the members of the commandos who still are living and we talk about what might have happened to Eddie.

Boy Scouts

During the Depression and subsequent war years, my siblings and I were kept constantly occupied with various chores, which we referred to as "jobs." Not only did Papa and Mama and Big Nonno and Little Nonna believe mightily in the virtue of hard work, they knew it kept us out of trouble. My brother Joseph and

I spent many years selling and delivering newspapers, mowing lawns, washing windows, shining shoes and working at various and sundry jobs, especially after we moved to the San Fernando Valley and were old enough to drive. Back in the neighborhood, our friends also were given various chores or jobs, but it seemed they never had as many as those meted out by Papa and Mama. There were many mouths to feed in our household with its seven kids, Mama, Papa, Big Nonno and Little Nonna and usually one or two other relatives who came to live with us during those hard economic times.

Although there was no shortage of ethnicity in our Dana Street neighborhood, there was little if any religious pluralism, except of course in the case of Eddie Hamil and his family. As far as we knew, the Hamils were not Catholic since we'd never seen them at St. Agnes, our neighborhood parish. The absence of religious diversity served to insulate us from the many different cultural opportunities provided to children of Protestants, such as Scouting, and it was only later that my siblings and I would come to know the richness and benefits resulting from living in the larger world.

So, it came as more than a little surprise when Eddie announced one afternoon that he was joining the newly established Boy Scout troop, which was meeting across the street from St. Agnes School.

We were playing marbles or "migs" as we called them when Eddie made his big announcement.

"Boy Scout troop? What's that?" we wanted to know.

We had never heard of a Boy Scout troop, let alone that one was being established across the street from our school on Adams Boulevard.

As we peppered Eddie with questions, he proceeded to sell us on the idea that we, too, could join the troop and become members of the Boy Scouts of America. We had to admit belonging to the B.S.A. held a great appeal for us, especially in those early years of World War II, even though we were unsure whether our parents would allow us to join. We told Eddie we would find out as soon as Joseph and I could ask Mama, who, in turn, would get Papa's approval.

When we asked Mama, she was reluctant to even consider our request.

"Didn't your friend Eddie tell you that the Boy Scouts are a Protestant group and that the Church doesn't allow Catholics to join?" she said.

"What?!!" We couldn't believe it.

"But Mama, the troop is meeting right across the street from our church," we countered.

"Well, we'll see," replied Mama.

We knew she would have to seek permission not only from Papa, but from Monsignor Maloney, the pastor of St. Agnes.

Finally, following two or three days of meetings, conferences and telephone calls, Mama announced we could join the local troop.

"Monsignor Maloney said it was okay to join," said Mama, "so long as you and Joseph continue to serve Mass and receive the sacraments."

"Whoopee!!" we yelled, darting out the back door to meet Art, Joey, Walter and Eddie.

We agreed that with our parents' and Monsignor Maloney's blessing, we would approach Mr. Blake, the new Troop master, later that week and ask to join Boy Scout Troop 011.

"Well, boys" said Mr. Blake when we finally met him, "you understand there are various rules and requirements you will be obliged to fulfill, don't you?"

"Sure, no problem, Sir," we replied.

And so began an arduous journey to learn the rudiments and requirements of Scouting, including memorizing the Boy Scout oath, tying knots, dressing in the standard B.S.A. uniform and earning merit badges. Most challenging of all was learning first aid, but that was a lesson we would learn right on the streets of our neighborhood.

Little by little, with each of us helping one another, we arrived at the point when we were sworn in as Boy Scouts of America Troop 011. Soon we would be earning our first merit badges.

Every second Thursday at 7 p.m., we'd hike to the empty lot adjacent to the Boy Scout cabin and wait for Mr. Blake and the start of our meeting. With 10 or 15 minutes to spare, we'd get a pickup baseball game going, using broom handles for bats and a couple of golf-ball-sized rocks for balls. On one particular evening as we played, setting sun behind the trees at the end of the lot gradually plunged us into darkness and it started to become difficult for us to follow the path of the "ball" as it was thrown overhand from the pitcher to the batter.

It was soon my turn at bat. I took a couple of practice swings and walked to home plate.

"Okay, lemme see a fast one down the middle," I yelled, straining to follow the trajectory of the stone as it left the pitcher's hand.

Squinting in the dimming light, I thought, "Where is it?" just as the rock struck me smack in the middle of my head, slicing my forehead open. Blood gushed into my eyes and past my nose and down I went, falling into a heap in front of home plate.

"He's down! Hey, Louie's been hit!" yelled Art.

"Here's Mr. Blake! Someone get the first aid kit so we can bandage him up," Walt and Art called out in unison.

As I lay on the ground, bleeding profusely from my forehead, at least eight or nine Scouts were screaming orders to each other. Soon, water and towels were applied to the wound where a bump the size of a small apricot was forming. Two, three and then more Scouts began applying iodine to the gauze and bandage on my eyes, head and forehead.

Mr. Blake shouted for a couple of Scouts to get the stretcher from the Scout Hut. As they eased me onto the stretcher, Mr. Blake calmly told four or five of the Scouts to carry me to my home on Dana Street, just around the corner. As the good Scouts approached the front porch of my home, Eddie said, "Hold it, I'll tell Mrs. Vaccaro what happened since I'm the oldest."

When Mama opened the door and saw me, she turned pale as a ghost.

"What happened?" she shrieked.

Eddie recounted the whole story, not leaving out a single detail. Mama was horrified.

"How am I ever going to tell Papa what happened?" she gasped.

"Aw," replied Eddie, "It ain't **that** bad. He'll be okay and besides, this 'accident' will help us qualify for our first merit badge in emergency first aid!"

Oh, great, I thought, you guys get your first aid badge and I catch hell from Papa!

Saturday Matinee

Another Saturday, we decided to trek up to the Adams Movie Theatre to scavenge in the trash bins and see if we could find any intact movie tickets. It often happened that the usher at the theater entrance would not entirely tear movie tickets into two pieces before discarding them in the trash bin. So, scavenging in the trash barrel out back often yielded one or more somewhat intact tickets, which was just like finding cash. Joseph was reminding us of this opportunity as we made our way to the Adams Movie Theater. We rarely walked directly anywhere—there were dozens of diversions, shortcuts and stops to poke around vacant lots and abandoned cars and check out "help wanted" signs in storefront shops, where a 10- or 11-year-old boy could sometimes find work.

As the Adams came into view, we raced toward the back, heading straight for the trash barrels to see who could find the hidden treasure of unused, partly torn movie tickets. Eddie went straight for a huge moving van parked in the rear lot of the theater. Walt, Joey and I made a beeline for the truck cab, seeing who could reach the steering wheel and gearshift first. We took turns at the wheel of the huge van, honking its horn while Eddie proceeded to open the back doors and dive in for a look.

"Holy crap," Eddie hollered. "Get back here! Call the cops!"

We scrambled down from the cab and ran to the rear. Eddie was straddling the body of what appeared to be a drunk.

"No," Eddie yelled. "He ain't drunk—he's dead! Call the cops, we'll get a reward!"

I ran around to the front of the theater, stopping by a small shop and telling the shopkeeper we had found "a dead guy." As the shopkeeper was dialing the police, I returned the truck to find Eddie rifling through the dead man's pockets. He found a book of matches, two partly-smoked cigarettes and one shiny nickel. Not content with emptying the pockets, Eddie showed us how he could punch the wino, producing strangle noises and snorts from the corpse.

The police car arrived with blaring sirens and flashing lights and Eddie immediately took charge.

"Hey, my name is Eddie Hamil and I found this guy," he said. "What kind of reward do I get?"

As the officers went about taking notes, snapping pictures and making measurements, Joey, Walt, Joseph and I stood aside, letting Eddie take center stage. The lead officer took out his wallet, handed Eddie his card and said, "This is the only reward we can give you—if you ever need help, just call us."

Eddie stood there, disappointed and dumbfounded, clutching an L.A. Police Department card with the officer's name and badge number. We dared not laugh, so we bit our tongues and held our breaths, waiting for Eddie's response.

"Hey," quipped Eddie, "How can you guys claim to be L.A.'s finest when you don't even offer rewards for our doing all your work?"

The cops just laughed as they beckoned to Eddie.

"Here," said the sergeant in charge as he handed Eddie a shiny half dollar, "Here's a reward. Take your buddies to the malt shop and treat yourselves to Cokes or ice cream bars."

Joseph goes up for a basket in 1953 at Valley Junior College.

Lou with Little Nonna.

Brother Michael with Little Nonna and Big Nonno

Chapter 4
At the Corner

I also vividly recall the times we would steal the wine bottle of our beloved Oscar, the older alcoholic news vendor who took over the "Corner" at the same time Joseph and I finished selling the late afternoon newspapers before heading home for dinner. Of course, we always saw to it that Oscar's bottle was always returned to him. Close to the "Corner" was "Johnnie's Candy Store." Johnnie was an older German man with limited English skills and very poor eyesight. Joseph and I and the other Commandos would frequent his candy store, visiting two or three times a week. The store was known for its penny candy and three-cent ice cream cones. Three cents for ice cream cones! It was unbelievable!

From 1941 to 1943, the U.S. Mint began minting pennies without copper. The pennies came out shiny silver, similar to dimes. We Commandos made a game of seeing how many shiny new pennies we could pass off as dimes at Johnnie's store. We would regularly gather up 10 pieces of penny candy and pay Johnnie one bright, shiny, newly-minted silver penny. Of course, with his poor eyesight, Johnnie thought it was a dime!

We were lucky we were never arrested or worse. If Papa ever caught on to what we were doing, there would have been hell to pay for sure!

Another time, Joseph, me and our cousin Bobbie Maron were walking through the Dana Street Elementary School playground when we stumbled upon our cousins Eddie and Dickie Maron. They were hiding behind a garage on the edge of the playground, smoking cigarettes. When they spotted us, they immediately motioned for us to join them to "smoke a weed." Joseph and I immediately refused. We knew Papa would kill us if he found out, even though Papa was a two-pack-a-day Camels smoker.

"Come on, you jerks," said Dickie. "If you won't smoke one, at least hold it and pretend."

"Well, okay," we agreed. He passed us a lighted Lucky Strike.

So we took a lit cigarette and held it as if we were puffing. Sure enough, along came the playground director, Mr. Wheeler.

"What in the world! What are you Vaccaro boys up to?" he asked.

Without time to protest, we were marched to our home down Dana Street. My mother answered the door and immediately wanted to know what had happened. There was no time to explain.

"Wait till Papa gets home!" Mama exclaimed. "You're in big trouble now."

Dinner with the family was a time to eat and never a time to talk. Talking was strictly forbidden by Papa. Following dinner, Virgie would wash the dishes and Joseph and I would dry them. No questions were ever asked and no complaints ever voiced. It was what it was.

When Papa did arrive home, nothing happened. Joseph and I felt we'd gotten a reprieve. No punishment awaited us. We went straight to bed after dinner. Evidently, Mama did not tell Papa a thing.

The next morning as we were preparing for school, Papa was at the table having his coffee and a cigarette.

"Well, you boys need to get your things together and leave so you will not be late for school," he said.

Joseph and I quickly grabbed our books, our lunches and headed for the door.

"What a minute," Papa called. "Haven't you forgotten something?"

"No," we said. "We have our books, our lunch boxes, our gym shoes—we're good to go."

"Come here." Papa beckoned as he reached into his shirt pocket and pulled out an unopened pack of Camels. "I think you will need these."

Oh, my God! Mama *did* tell him, we thought as we cried our way to school.

But it worked. Neither Joseph nor I ever touched a cigarette until I began smoking in 1951, the year I enlisted in the U.S. Air Force.

As it happened, the day Papa died, December 13, 1963, I smoked my last cigarette. I finally proved to myself I no longer needed Papa's permission.

"American Day" play at Dana Street Elementary School in 1937. Pictured are Virgie (back row, left), two classmates and in the front row, Joseph, Michael and Lou.

Mama (center) with Joseph, Michael, Lou and Virgie at the park in Los Angeles, 1936.

Chapter 5
Childhood Lessons

During those Depression years, we also shared our large home with my paternal aunt, Ellen Vaccaro Wheeler, who was dying of cancer when I was nine years old. In 1941, my mother's sister, Philomena "Minnie" Maron, her husband, Edward or "Eddie;" and their five children also moved in with us after leaving upstate New York, where they had lost everything. In those days, family was one place you could go to get back on your feet and for the Maron family, they were able to start all over by living with us until they could afford their own apartment. This busy household provided plenty of warm and loving relationships between grandparents, aunts, uncles and cousins.

It also provided a classroom of sorts, where I could learn about life.

My father, for example, was tough, demanding and authoritarian. We never questioned when he told us to do something—we just did it. And it was from him I learned the virtues of hard work, honesty, self-discipline, responsibility and devotion to family. Although neither of my parents told us they loved us, they showed their affection in other ways, in the way they provided for us and made us toe the mark. We knew we were loved.

I tried hard to follow my father's advice to work with my head and not my hands. I wanted to be a good student at St. Agnes—a scholar even—but my antics with the Commandos often took time away from my studies. Eventually, it caught up with me. I failed the third grade and was held back. My brother Joseph joined me there the following year and we spent the rest of our school careers in the same grade, graduating together from Van Nuys High School in 1949.

.I wanted desperately to show that I could make something of myself. Exasperated with my daydreaming, Papa used to call me many unflattering names. In his eyes, I wasn't quick enough. I was more of a dreamer and a thinker while my brother Joseph was the one who was quick. I would think first about the best way to do something. Joseph would act. My father preferred quick action. He often wondered why I couldn't be more like Joseph.

High Mass Hijinks

Young boys from age 8 also were expected to serve at Mass at St. Agnes Church. One of my earliest memories was when Joseph and I were recruited to be altar servers for Mass at St. Agnes.

Daily mass was a given at St. Agnes. If you were enrolled in grades 1-12, you had better show up—or else! "Or else" meant facing the music from Sister Rita Charles. Actually, among the guys, all of whom were members of the Dana Street Commandos, Sister Rita Charles was referred to as "Sister Rigor Mortis." It was not that she was mean or cruel—we saw her as big, stern and strong. Not only did Sister Rita Charles teach fourth grade, she was also in charge of the Altar Boys, so even before the formation of the Dana Street Commandos, we were saddled with someone who was more or less a towering "commander-in-chief."

To our eyes, Sister Rita Charles was huge. Or so she appeared to the five of us who comprised our small clique in the fourth grade. Art, Walter, Joey, my brother Joseph and me were also known as "The Unholy Five," to Sister Rita Charles.

One day, just prior to the end of class, our "Commander in Chief" announced she wanted Arthur, Joey, Walter, Joseph and "Louis" to stay after class. We were terrified. Such an order would not have come unless one of us had messed up and was unaware of it. We looked at each other as if to ask, "Okay, now what? Who did it? Oh man, here we go again!" After everyone had filed out of the classroom on the second floor of our "prison," as we often referred to our school, we sat quietly and attentively, waiting for the hammer to drop, all the while studying our commander as she paced before the blackboard, fingering her rosary beads. Her huge rosary beads were attached to a thick belt encircling her towering body. Then in a move we had to admire, this large but graceful fourth-grade teacher bellowed out, "How many of you know what a High Mass is?" Silence. Not a peep from any of The Unholy Five.

Of course, we knew what Mass was since we were obliged to attend every day and on weekends but a "High Mass?" We didn't have a clue! So, Sister Rita proceeded to lecture and indoctrinate us on the origin and significance of celebrating a High Mass. We still had no clue what she wanted from us. As it turned out, toward the end of her lecture, she explained she wanted each of us to learn to serve the High Mass, but in our serving we would be relegated to serving as "sanctuary boys." We quickly found out that we five would join with another group of 19 sanctuary boys and that we would be required to sit, kneel and stand facing the altar as the priest and various related altar servers performed their duties during the 90 minutes it took to celebrate the High Mass. So, as she wound down her lecture, Sister Rita said she wanted us to meet her in the sanctuary of the church every day after class for the next week. At that time, she would instruct us on our responsibilities and how we will be expected to comport ourselves during the celebration of the High Mass. The next day, we met our commander and she began step-by-step, move–by –move, article-by-article to instruct us on how we were expected to comport ourselves as sanctuary boys for the celebration of the High Mass. All the while excitement mixed with apprehension was building a level of tension in our small pre-adolescent minds.

"Now, I expect you to show up, prepared and dressed properly for the Mass, one half hour before the Mass begins at 11am on Sunday," Sister Rita told us on the final day of our instructions. "Number one, wash your face and *especially* behind your ears, clean your fingernails, wear a white shirt and tie, and please wear dark trousers and dark socks. Do you understand?"

We never knew she had the word "Please" in her vocabulary. I was somewhat relieved when we left St. Agnes Church and headed to our neighborhood haunts to further discuss and complain about what was being required of us at our first High Mass. When we got home, of course, we informed our mothers and as one might suspect, they were thrilled beyond belief that their boys had been selected to serve as "sanctuary boys at High Mass at St. Agnes Church." Before we knew it, Sunday morning arrived and each of us performed our required washing and cleaning rituals.

My brother Joseph and I stopped by Joey's house and the three of us met with Walter and Art at the sanctuary entrance of the church. We were not prepared for the military-like plan and precision formulated by Sister Rita Charles. Sister Rita was a hard taskmaster but she got the job done and she really did love her altar boys.

So, here she was, barking out orders, pacing up and down the dressing room, occasionally twisting the ear of an errant young boy and generally making it known she was, in fact, "commander-in-chief." As sanctuary boys, we were required to wear black patent leather shoes and a red cassock over our white shirts, to which was attached another starched white collar. When Sister Rita Charles affixed that white collar, you can bet she was inspecting the cleanliness of each of our ears. Then we were required to don a white lace surplice. Now, the Unholy Five were dressed as sacristy choirboys, joining the other nineteen sanctuary boys, all of whom were older and taller than us. We were then required to line up by height in two rows so all twenty-four were divided into two lines of twelve sanctuary boys each.

"Alright, each of you knows what to do," bellowed Sister Rita. "You have been trained and prepared so don't embarrass me or the Holy Cross Sisters of St. Agnes School."

As we began our procession into the main altar area, we took our places in front of the hard wooden benches facing the altar of the church. Following us were Monsignor Mahoney, Father Moran and five or six other altar servers, including the master of ceremonies and the one who had the coolest job—preparing and using the incense servers.

"I approach the altar of God, God the joy of my youth," the High Mass began in Latin.

As instructed, we stood and knelt and sat on cue. As we were sitting for the fifth time, I glanced to my right and noticed my buddy Joey Blankmeyer fidgeting with his nose. Now Joey was the ideal-looking altar boy. He was about five feet tall with blond curly hair and blue eyes. I looked at him intently and whispered, "Why are you picking your nose?"

Somewhat irritated, he replied, "Because I think I'm having a bloody nose!"

"Well, my gosh, Joey," I said in hushed tones, "get your handkerchief out and plug your nose to stop the flow of the blood! You've got blood all over your surplice!"

He proceeded to apply his white handkerchief, which immediately became drenched in blood. More than a little concerned, I turned to him again and whispered again in heightened tones, "Go up and get out of here and go into the outer dressing room so someone can take care of you. Sister Rita is out there and she will help you."

"Geez, I can't do that," Joey replied. "Sister Rita will kill me!"

What a choice! Bleed to death or be killed by Sister Rita Charles!

And so began our first experience serving "High Mass."

Chapter 6
Codes of Conduct

V ermont and Adams was less than a mile from the campus of the University of Southern California, where Lou would later earn his bachelor's degree in economics and social sciences and a master's degree in the history and philosophy of education.

"Papa" kept them busy hawking papers at the corner and Lou and Joseph were enterprising enough to also set up a shoeshine business, which they pursued up and down Vermont Avenue, close to the USC campus. He made his own shoeshine box while spending less than $2 for brushes and supplies. It proved to be a lucrative business; Lou and Joseph were able to station themselves near the saloons and bars on Vermont where there was heavy foot traffic. They also sneaked into the saloons to ply their trade to the many half-drunk patrons. Eventually, Lou and Joseph acquired their own two-seater shoeshine stand when the Vaccaro family moved to Tarzana in the San Fernando Valley. The shoeshine stand was located in the PX of the airbase at the Van Nuys Airport. Lou's boss was an African-American minister known as "Deacon Jones."

The Depression years were tough for everyone, but we were fortunate to have a large back yard on Dana

Street where we raised chickens for eggs and meat. We also raised rabbits and Little Nonna cultivated a large vegetable garden in the back yard.

My grandmother was the predominant religious person in our family. She got up every morning at 5 a.m., walked the two blocks to St. Agnes Church and opened the doors so the priest could come in and celebrate Mass. My mother also was religious and our entire family except my father and grandfather regularly attended Mass and other services at St. Agnes.

Irish Catholic priests from the old country, headed by Monsignor Mahony and Father Moran, staffed the parish. Father Moran was another tough hombre. Whenever he wanted work done in the parish, he would come after my brother Joseph and me and our buddies. We were regularly recruited to set up tables and chairs for card parties and Bingo games. Our lives were not devoid of bosses.

Meanwhile, at the school, the Sisters of the Holy Cross called on Louis Sr. when any work projects needed to be done.

My father was not an overtly religious man, but he was a highly moral person. He would regularly fix the plumbing and do various repairs in the classrooms for the sisters. He was never paid for the work but it was duly noted when my parents were faced with tuition bills. Oftentimes these were forgiven or whittled down.

I had many good role models among my extended family. I remember my cousin, Anthony Furtivo, whose mother was my aunt, Angeline Vaccaro D'Amico. Anthony was an important role model for me when I was growing up. Around 1940-41, he held the United States high school record for the 100-yard dash while attending University High School in Los Angeles. He was also a gifted artist and musician. He played piano, drums and guitar. Eventually, he went on to earn a degree in art from the Los Angeles Art Institute and later worked as a graphic design artist for one of America's leading toy manufacturers. I idolized my cousin Anthony. He was the older brother I never had.

My more formal classroom lessons were provided by some of my favorite teachers at St. Agnes School, Van Nuys High School and throughout college and university studies. I recall with great fondness Sister Mary Luke, third grade teacher at St. Agnes and the most memorable Sister Luke's practice of reading aloud to our class every Friday afternoon. Her favorite and mine was "Winnie the Pooh." She had a knack of embellishing her readings with impersonations and sound effects. She really could have given Carol Burnett a run for the money!

Of all my grade school teachers, I most recall the time I spent sitting spellbound in Sister Luke's third grade classroom.

In addition to regaling us with "Winnie the Pooh" stories and drilling into our heads the elements of proper English, math and history, Sister Luke introduced us to the needs of the Pagan Babies. Pagan Babies were children who had been abandoned or orphaned in places like China, India and Africa. Missionaries had set up societies to rescue, care for and baptize these babies. Sister Luke encouraged us to save our pennies and place them in the little cardboard boxes designed to look like miniature Chinese houses. At the end of the month, the boxes were collected and turned into Sister Luke. She would send the boxes on to the principal of the school and tell us that we had done a very good thing for both the Chinese children and the Church in "that pagan land." Of course, Joseph, Virgie, and me would do what we could and we felt good doing our share. Little did I realize at the time just how closely connected I would become to the people of China. Forty years later, in 1980, I would begin visiting China and eventually become a teacher, adviser and friend to thousands of Chinese adult college students and teachers. My experiences resulted in helping more than 300 Chinese students travel to the U.S. for their college and university studies.

I often wonder if any of these students or their families were helped through the pagan babies' campaign largesse. It just might have happened!

Dinner time with Joseph.

In the U.S. Air Force, Bangor, Maine.

With buddy Bill in Bangor at Dow AFB.

Lou and Pat Palmer, Siena Heights College (now University) 1980

Conferring with officials from New London, New Hampshire about Colby-Sawyer College in 1974.

Chapter 7
The War Years and Beyond

D ecember 7, 1941 was an unforgettable Sunday. I remember after Joseph and I finished delivering papers, we were visiting Walt Reardan. While we were standing out in the street in front of Walt's apartment building, an older man stopped and asked us if we'd heard the news.

"What news?" we asked.

"The Japs have just bombed Pearl Harbor," said the stranger.

He advised us to hurry home.

We all huddled around the Philco radio, listening to broadcasts bringing the news from Hawaii. From that moment on, we followed the daily events that brought us to war with Japan and the war against the Germans in Europe. And because we delivered the papers every day, we were able to read first-hand about the events in Europe and the Pacific Theater.

Not long after the attack on Pearl Harbor, we saw an Army truck with several soldiers stopping in front of Mr. Parker's drug store on the corner of Dana Street and Vermont Avenue. Very quickly and in an official way, the soldiers tacked up a notice on the telephone pole announcing that all Japanese aliens in that area were to begin packing their personal belongings and be ready to be shipped out to detention camps on the

West Coast within one week. This was the controversial executive order signed by FDR, aimed at isolating any person of Japanese heritage, even those who were U.S. citizens, moving them from all areas in the U.S. and imprisoning them in various detention camps located in Oregon, Washington, Idaho, and California. Later that week, we viewed first hand some of the Vaccaro neighbors of Japanese descent packed into large army trucks with their baggage, suitcases, and belongings, never to be seen again. Those images plague me to this day.

Within two years, the Vaccaro family was making its own move to Tarzana, where "Papa" became a wholesale distributor for the Los Angeles Times and Lou and his siblings started a new chapter in their lives, away from the childhood security of the Dana Street neighborhood.

It became increasingly difficult for me to leave my childhood friends behind and move to Tarzana, 40 miles away. Tarzana was rural farmland dotted with fig trees and walnut orchards. At the Tarzana Elementary School, I remember having the chance to play Joseph in the Christmas Tableau at school and I met Patty Gump, who played Mary. She was a perky, cute blonde, and I somehow imagined a romantic relationship might be possible until she revealed to me she was not Catholic.

Our home there had three bedrooms and one bath. The move to the valley meant I eventually would go from Catholic to public school. Joseph and I started seventh grade together at Tarzana Elementary School and completed eighth grade at St. Elizabeth School. In short order, we were going onto the high school.

The move from parochial grade school to Van Nuys High School was a tough transition. Much larger, VNHS had at least 4,000 students, many of whom were not Catholic and from every walk of life. Some well-known graduates of Van Nuys included: Marilyn Monroe, Tom Selleck, Natalie Wood, Don Drysdale,

Robert Redford, Dion Dow, brother of Tony Dow of "Leave it to Beaver" fame, and Jane Russell. Many others not named here went on to television, movie and sports fame.

But to their classmates, they were just ordinary kids and we all benefitted from a great group of teachers in the years following the end of World War II. Two of my favorite teachers were actually coaches: Jack Mclintock, who coached baseball, and Barney Quinn who coached basketball. Mr. Quinn stands out because he invited his good friend, Johnnie Wooden of UCLA fame when Coach Wooden had just begun his phenomenal run as America's winningest basketball coach for the UCLA Bruins. Coach McLintock stands out because he gave me the chance to play for his very talented baseball team and in fact, tapped me to pitch against the UCLA freshman team in 1949. I can't recall if we won or not. McLintock later coached Don Drysdale, which led to Drysdale's success in Major League Baseball with the Los Angeles Dodgers.

Papa later became a wholesale distributor for the *Los Angeles Times* so Joseph and I were roused from a sound sleep every morning at 4 o'clock to sell newspapers in the patient wards at the Birmingham Army Hospital and the Van Nuys Airport air base. After we finished at 7:30 a.m., we returned home for breakfast and then went on to school. The hospital housed veterans of the Pacific Theater who had been injured and were returning home, while the airport housed the P-38 and Black Widow fighter squadrons. Eventually Joseph and I would be known as the newspaper boys around the base as well as the sons of "Louie" Vaccaro. We also were working our way up to becoming self-employed shoeshine boys, eventually owning our own two-seater stand.

By 1943, we were outgrowing our Tarzana home. There were nine people sharing three bedrooms and one bath and it was getting cramped. Then, my mother found a large house on Gilmore Street in Van

Nuys. At first, my father wasn't keen on the idea of the house. He didn't think we could afford it. But my mother was able to get the woman who owned it to sell it for $9,000. My father's friend Joe Ross loaned him the money interest-free. The house needed a lot of work, but that wasn't a problem since my father was a plumber by trade and we all began working to repair the house. When we moved to Gilmore Street, Little Nonna came to live with us as did my father's single brother, Mike, who was suffering with cancer. He had moved west from his job in Pittsburgh.

From our new house, it was about a three-quarter-mile walk to Van Nuys High School and our new elementary school, St. Elizabeth's. It was around that time that Joseph and I started developing our shoeshine business, going from barracks to barracks, officers' mess hall to officers' club, shining the shoes of the servicemen on the base. That first summer, a black man dressed like a minister and chauffeured by a young white woman in a Cadillac convertible invited us to work for him. His name was "Deacon Jones." He said he had a "good deal" for us. He would set us up with our own shoeshine stand. We would charge 15 cents for each pair of shoes, we would keep 10 cents and he'd get 5 cents. He said he was experienced in setting up shoeshine parlors. Since we couldn't keep our newspaper money—we turned that over to our parents to help support our family—we jumped at the opportunity. Even though we charged 15 cents per shine, we'd often get 10-cent tips. On schedule, Deacon Jones would come around every week to collect his share of our earnings. One day, he didn't show up and after waiting another month, we learned he'd been arrested. So Joseph and I ended up owning the two-seater shoeshine stand—a good deal, indeed!

At Birmingham Hospital, when we had time between the morning and afternoon papers, we'd make extra money as pinsetters at the hospital bowling alley. The hospital became the setting for the film, "The Men," starring Marlon Brando and we were delighted to have the opportunity eventually to see some of the places we frequented appear in the movie.

During the Second World War years, my brothers Joseph, Michael and I all would sell papers at the hospital, the air base, at the church on Sunday mornings and also deliver them throughout the San Fernando Valley. One day, when Joseph and I were coming home from school, we were told by Papa to change into our work clothes and were met by wheelbarrows, shovels, hoes and a pick. We were trained not to ask "why."

"I'm going to begin shoveling out dirt from the crawlspace under the house and you boys are going to shovel it from the driveway into the wheelbarrow and cart it to the back yard so we can level it off," Papa told us.

Over the next two years, we dug a full basement from a small crawlspace. The cellar had been transformed to a room with a concrete floor and solid walls. Later, a couple friends who had trouble at home and needed a place to stay were allowed to move in. Tommy Levine and Eddie Taylor came to live with us and used the basement as a bedroom for about six months.

After the war years, Joseph and I were in our third year of high school. At that time, we qualified for our driver's licenses and we began to drive the delivery trucks for Papa from one end of the valley to the other. As the business grew, we were assembling and delivering 36,000 copies of the LA Times each weekend. Of course, there were other jobs, too.

Papa was not in favor of our playing sports be- cause if we were injured, we couldn't work and contribute to the family income. But, we sneaked out and did it anyway. I played baseball while Joseph was the better basketball player. Academically, I had a number of inspirational and motivational teachers and because I was the son of Italian immigrants, I was steered toward the industrial arts curriculum. The teacher who was one of my earliest favorites was Mr. Lynch, who taught general science. Another was my shop teacher, Mr. Saunders.

My best friends in high school were Herbie Reyes and Bertram Nitsch. We hung out and talked every day during the lunch break. Bert would suggest double dates frequently but I was petrified to ask a girl out on a date. Finally, I got my courage up and asked a cute girl to go out with me. I think her name was Janice. At the last minute, Bert changed his mind so I had to be by myself on my first date. I had promised Janice I would pick her up and we would meet Bert and his date. Frantic, I had to find a way out of it. Finally, I called Janice and told her I had my license taken away for getting a traffic ticket. To this day, I feel so guilty about lying to this girl and to this day, Bert and I talk about it and he just laughs. It was yet another of life's lessons.

After my first year in junior college, I joined the Air Force so I wouldn't be drafted. It was the beginning of the Korean War and about three times more recruits showed up at Lackland AFB than expected so we were shipped out to Lockbourn AFB in Columbus, Ohio. Eventually, we landed at Selfridge Air Force Base, close to Detroit, Michigan. Selfridge was a temporary assignment to prepare us to be shipped to the East Coast. Ultimately, I found myself stationed at Dow AFB in Bangor, Maine. I had never been that far east in my life, never had been in that cold a climate and never experienced a culture quite like Maine.

While stationed at Dow AFB, I was helping Major Reginald Hayes move his living quarters from one side of the base to the other, and I sustained a severe back injury. During my month-long hospital stay, I met Lieutenant Lois Algren, a gem of a nurse from Sioux City, Iowa, and we began dating.

I was starting to learn the ropes in the Air Force, and I passed the flight school test at the air base in

Rome, New York and then was placed on a waiting list. My experiences were giving me more confidence when dealing with members of the opposite sex. The result was I dated a lot more and learned more about myself and what I wanted to do.

Lou gets together with high school and college buddies, 1950-51, L.A. Valley College.

Lou at his first commencement in 1967 at the University of Portland as the school's first lay vice president.

Chapter 8
Choices

B ut, family responsibilities beckoned again. My father was suffering financially and in declining health so in 1953 I received a hardship discharge and returned home to help support my family once again. I started back to school part-time at L.A. Valley College and worked full-time to support the Vaccaro clan. While at the college, I joined the Newman Club and met Jean Hudak, who I would eventually marry. I earned my associate's degree in liberal arts and was admitted to the University of Southern California.

While in college, my interest in philosophy and theology, both areas that were well suited to my introspective nature, blossomed. What would I do after graduation? Following my discharge, I was eligible for the Korean G.I. Bill and an assessment test revealed public relations as a perfect fit for me. The woman administering the test recommended I go to the best journalism school I could find and that happened to be the University of Southern California. So, I drove the 50 miles round trip to USC every other day and planned to finish school in 1957 or 1958.

There's an old adage that life is what happens while you're making other plans. Such was the case for me because somewhere along the way, Jean and I decided to get married. In January 1955 at St. Elisabeth Church in Van Nuys, we tied the knot. My uncle, Mike Vince, who attended the wedding, talked us into traveling back to Buffalo so I could work with him and finish my degree at the University of Buffalo. At the end of our first year there, we discovered we were going to become parents. Jean wanted to be near her family so we moved back to California in 1956 and I re-enrolled at USC. Our daughter Mary Louise was born March 16, 1956. "Mary Lou" was followed by Therese Jean on June 13, 1957; Victoria Ann, October 5, 1959; Frances Paula, December 22, 1961; Michelle Marie, October 26, 1963; and Justin Louis, October 28, 1969.

Having a wife and children meant finding a job so I started working at Pacific Bell Telephone and Telegraph Company and attending graduate school at Cal State Northridge. I didn't really enjoy my work at Pacific Bell, although there were many opportunities to advance within the organization. Graduate school made me realize I wanted to be a teacher, I wanted to help others and impact their lives in a positive way, to show them the opportunities that awaited them with a good education. Once my master's degree was finished, I spent a year teaching at Cal State, I was convinced college teaching really *was* my perfect fit. Just around the corner from my first year of teaching at Cal State was a one-year teaching assignment at St. Mary's College in South Bend, Indiana.

And so my career in higher education was launched.

Jim Ebben, academic vice president and provost at Siena Heights University in the 1970s and 80s, and his wife, Marilyn.

Lou welcoming Steve Allen to Siena Heights College in the fall of 1979. Allen and his wife, Jayne Meadows, spent three days on campus and were awarded honorary degrees. They brought their acclaimed PBS program, "Meeting of the Minds" to the Adrian, Michigan college and were joined by several professors in a staging of the popular show.

Conferring with the president of the John Deere Corporation and the publisher of the Davenport, Iowa newspaper about the plans for the new nursing building at Marycrest College in 1971.

Chapter 9
Learning the Ropes

In 1961, we moved to East Lansing so I could finish my doctorate. We lived in Spartan Village on the campus of Michigan State University and met our good friends Wally and Nan Ewing and their four daughters.

Dr. Wallace Ewing remembers, "I enrolled at Michigan State University in the fall of 1962 to complete my bachelor degree requirements. Lou was starting the last year of his work toward his doctorate. I was an English major and he was writing his doctoral thesis. Beyond our educational pursuits, we each had four daughters, we lived next to each other in Spartan Village, a married housing complex at the university, we were about the same age, our children were similar in ages, and our wives soon became close friends. Our lives blended beautifully, both professionally and socially. Neither of us had much money, but we shared family activities and our friendship became closer and closer in the process. It is still strong 48 years later."

With two master's degrees and additional post-graduate coursework under my belt, I discovered I could finish my coursework in three semesters at MSU. I declared higher education as my main field of study with a cognate in sociology. I began with a vengeance to take as many courses as possible to finish my doctorate. I was determined to complete my program as soon as possible.

Many fine professors influenced my graduate studies. Max Smith, my major professor, was a very formal individual. Other members of my doctoral committee included Dr. Al Eldersveld, Professor Bill Roe, who I had met while teaching at St. Mary's, and Dr. Iwao Ishino, who taught sociology and was someone I admired very much. Dr. Ed Blackman was the assistant dean in the College of Education and had been a classmate of Joseph Kennedy Jr. Ed Blackman was a distinguished professor of the classics, Latin and Greek, before becoming the assistant dean in the College of Education. He was among my most challenging and satisfying professors. He eventually directed my dissertation and was very easy to work with. We saw eye to eye on most educational topics. He was a true mentor.

While at MSU, I was named a W.K. Kellogg Fellow. During my final term, I traveled to the Parker House Hotel in Chicago for the American Association for Higher Education conference. Because our funds were limited, four of us shared a room. One of my roommates was Bud Goodwin from West Virginia. While I was out attending panels and talks, he stayed in the room, studying. One afternoon, when I returned, he said a man named John Raynor had been calling all day. Since I didn't know anyone named John Raynor, I thought I should call back right away. I dialed the number Bud had scribbled down. A gentleman answered.

"This is John Raynor, what can I do for you?" he asked.

"This is Lou Vaccaro," I said. "I heard you've been trying to reach me."

A Jesuit priest, Father John Raynor was the vice president for academic affairs at Marquette University in Milwaukee, Wisconsin. He told me he had gotten my name from another person attending the conference, who had told him I might be in the market for a job. Father Raynor said he was interested in talking to me about some opportunities at Marquette. At the time, I told him I was working on my dissertation—it was March—and I thought I'd be finished around July or August.

We had a two-hour visit. He gave me some background on himself and we talked about his vision for the university. He had been at Marquette for about 18 months and had five jobs open he wanted to talk to me about. So, Jean and I made the trip to Milwaukee soon after, bringing Frannie and Vicki along for a two-day visit to the Marquette campus. I was introduced to a variety of people at the school and learned a little about each of the jobs that Father Raynor was hoping to fill. I went from office to office, interviewing deans and VPs, and learning

Father J.P. Raynor, S.J. Department of Special Collections and University Archives Marquette University Libraries.

about the Jesuit system of education and the opportunities at Marquette. Following the interviews, I was asked what I thought about each job and whether I had an interest in joining the Marquette community.

I was offered a position as assistant to Father Raynor, who later became president of the university. We moved to Milwaukee in 1963 and bought a three-bedroom house, close to Christ the King parish.

I had never been involved in an institution as large as Marquette University. There were ten colleges and schools, including engineering, medicine, business, dentistry, communications and liberal arts. I worked closely with Father Raynor, met with the board of trustees, worked on a variety of special projects and taught a class in the graduate school. The most rewarding project was developing a study abroad program with the University of Madrid.

I spent three satisfying years with Father Raynor and later with Bill Miller, an outstanding professor and biographer of Dorothy Day. Soon after I had passed that three-year mark, I learned about a post-doctoral fellowship at the Center for Advanced Study of Educational Administration at the University of Oregon. It was a yearlong program, and I was encouraged to apply, assured I would get my job back when I returned. We sold our home in Milwaukee, stored our furniture, took the train west and rented a home from a professor who was on sabbatical. Michelle had been born in Milwaukee, so there were the five girls on the train with Jean and I—they were all troopers. To this day, I marvel how we did it. Everyone was terrific. It was an adventure for all of us, moving to a furnished home in Eugene, Oregon. During our year at the University of Oregon, I completed additional coursework in community sociology and the sociology of organizations.

During this time, I wrote my first book, *New Perspectives in Catholic Higher Education.* My studies in Eugene happened during the Kennedy administration and because I was interested in going into the Peace Corps, I applied and was invited to visit Washington, D.C. While preparing to travel there, I talked to a good friend of mine in Oregon, a Chinese Benedictine monk, and told him I'd be flying through Portland on my way to Washington so we met for tea. Father Bernard Hwang discouraged me from going into the Peace Corps. As he put it, "You can't take your five daughters to Africa now! There will be other opportunities. We need you here."

Father Bernard informed me there was an opening for an academic vice president at the University of Portland. I applied and Father Paul Waldschmidt, C.S.C. made me an offer. At the time, the position paid $20,000 a year. I told him I would take the job but I didn't want to make more than the highest-paid faculty member. He was stunned but pleased, so we settled on $18,000. We bought a home across the Columbia River in Vancouver, Washington. It was my first position as a full-time administrator and I was the first layman to be appointed academic vice president. My experiences at the University of Portland led me to become good friends with a professor of history, James Covert. I began studying student demonstrations and the free speech movement, which erupted on many U.S. campuses. Because of my connections with colleagues at Stanford and Berkley, Professor Covert and I ended up putting together a book of essays with eight or nine other professors titled, "Student Freedom in American Higher Education." The book, published by Columbia University, received a number of positive reviews.

I spent three years at the University of Portland—it was a little like my own private post-doctoral experience. This was a time of great campus change—it was the height of campus revolution throughout the U.S. The book and my experience at Portland really opened many doors for me. I was inundated with opportunities to apply for presidencies at many Catholic colleges and universities. It was probably shortsighted of me at the time since a move meant uprooting our entire family once again—but I just couldn't say no.

Dr. Byron Doenges, left, deputy director of the U.S. Arms Control and Disarmament Agency, visited Colby College in New Hampshire on Nov. 20, 1974 to meet with his former colleague, Dr. Louis Vaccaro, president of Colby and Mrs. James Cleveland, associate professor in the social and behavioral sciences department. Mrs. Cleveland was married to congressman James Cleveland (R).

Chapter 10
Small Schools

After a couple of years, I took a presidency at Marycrest College in Davenport, Iowa. Once again, we packed our trunks and headed east to Rock Island, Illinois, which, with Davenport, Moline and East Moline, Illinois and Bettendorf, Iowa, forms the region known as the "Quad Cities."

Marycrest

Marycrest was an idyllic Catholic college with a lot of problems. My first task was to help it become truly co-educational. We did this by starting basketball and soccer sports programs. Later, we raised considerable funds for the college, including a $1 million federal grant to construct a new nursing building.

My other challenge was to preside over the merger of St. Ambrose College and Marycrest. It was the most intense period of work I've ever participated in, requiring eight to twelve hours a day, seven days a week. Our goal was to create a new institution, Newman College, which would include a new board of trustees and combined admissions office. Essentially, I wrote myself out of a job. I felt the president of Newman should be someone new and not from either

Marycrest or St. Ambrose. After the merger, I met a young, dynamic consultant from Boston who wanted to know whether I'd be interested in helping a small college for women in New London, New Hampshire. Because I was looking for a job, I applied, submitted my papers and was invited to Boston to interview with the trustees at the Copley Plaza Hotel.

Colby-Sawyer

The college and New London were decidedly Protestant. The college had been founded by Baptists and remained small. It was struggling. When Jean and I arrived, the Board of Trustees hosted a welcoming reception for us in the president's house, which had been built by the Colgate family across from the campus. We were a little nervous about the whole situation. After all, we were Catholic with a large family and decidedly not from New England. David Coffin of Connecticut was chairman of the board of trustees and an outstanding guy. He was very likeable and easy to get along with. We had several meetings and at the end of our two-day visit, he offered me the job. It paid $22,000 a year and housing was provided in the impressive Colgate mansion. We went back home to tell everyone we had accepted the new position. The girls and Jean, as usual, were just great about the whole move, although I'm sure they were reluctant to leave their friends in Rock Island and Davenport and it must have been hard for them.

When we arrived, we were met at the airport in Boston by Duke Rowe, the college chauffeur. We also were provided with a gardener and a housekeeper. One of the first things I had to do was lay off some of the staff since the school was having a very tough time financially and I didn't think it could continue to bear the expenses. Shortly after I became president of Colby, I contacted my old friend, Wally Ewing and invited him to New London. Wally later would become academic dean for the college.

Recalls Wally: "Lou is a people-oriented person. He likes people. He is concerned about the needy and the downtrodden. Lou always is willing to open his home to the down-and-out, to feed them, to shelter them, and to clothe them, if necessary. However, his good works do not stop there. Lou is equally concerned about helping students advance in their education pursuits, particularly the Chinese. He has placed in graduate

Wally and Jane Ewing

school several of the students who were in my classes when I taught in China and helped them find significant financial aid.

"Behind his altruism is his strong commitment to Christianity and his in-bred Catholicism. He is a firm believer, and that firmness shows in his self-confidence and leadership. He is a leader because there is no mistake that he leads. He listens to the opinions of others, but he is not afraid to make difficult decisions that may run contrary to popular positions.

"It's hard to imagine anyone less likely to be chosen president of Colby Junior College (now Colby-Sawyer), with his Italian heritage, Roman Catholicism, large family (six children at the time he became president of Colby Junior College), California roots, and Midwest ties. All this plunked on a small, conservative New Hampshire town with northern European ties. (Perhaps the Board of Trustees also deserves credit for making the tough choice.) As President, Lou was faced with declining enrollment, budget deficits, and a declining interest in the junior college philosophy. In a short time, he moved Çolby to a four-year school, despite a recalcitrant faculty and a few townspeople and alumnae who questioned his presence.

"At the time he was named President of Colby Junior, he asked me to apply for the job of Dean of the College. I was honored to be asked and doubly honored when I was appointed to that position. I don't think it was a question of "old boys" networking. He believed in me and what I would be able to do, a confidence that exceeded my own personal assessment. I think he was right, and I think his choice reveals his ability to read character and his desire to help others advance in their profession."

Every college has its own unique culture and every college culture is difficult to change. Colby-Sawyer, previously Colby Junior College for Women was no exception. Arriving there in 1972 from the Midwest, I found a typical New England college set in a typical New England town of about 2,500 souls. The college, founded 150 years earlier, had started as a co-ed academy and then transitioned to a two-year college for women. It thrived until the 1960s, then became stagnant in terms of enrollment and lost its allure for young 17-18-year-old women. After many meetings and conversations and a lot of observing, I believed a major change was needed. I suggested converting the college into a four-year liberal arts college by adding several baccalaureate programs and even changing the name.

We dropped the "Junior College" label and after lots of research and more meetings, we settled on Colby-Sawyer College in honor of the beloved president, Dr. Lesley Sawyer, who had transformed the academy into a two-year junior college for women.

I had my work cut out for me. We had to win over older alumnae and convince the trustees that it would work. Enrollment at Colby started growing after six or seven months and today the school is a thriving, well-respected and well-known institution throughout New England.

During my third year, I was asked to sign a 20-year contract by Bill Baird, the chairman emeritus of the board. But I just didn't want to be committed for 20 years and I didn't feel the college should commit to anyone for that period of time. While at Colby, I became active internationally, traveling to Greece with the school's alumni group and later to Brazil. I fell in love with both countries because they reminded me of California. I was publishing more, getting involved internationally on side trips to Brazil. But, after five or six years, it was apparent Jean was unhappy there and it was time to move on once again.

Perhaps my experience at Colby might have been easier if I had been a graduate of a New England "ivy league" school and not someone from "out west" with the added baggage of a large family and no New England connections. The road was often rough, but well worth traveling.

Siena Heights

In the mid-1970s, I started looking for another job and found Siena Heights in Adrian, Michigan. Marilyn Ebben, wife of Jim Ebben, met me at Detroit Metropolitan Airport. I interviewed with Sister Carmela O'Connor, affectionately known as "Sister Carmie," Anne Brown, and the rest of the Adrian Dominicans. After a short time, I was offered the position and I accepted, knowing Jean wanted to get out of New London. We moved in August 1977. My first feelings at Siena Heights were that I felt out of my element, working in such a vastly different environment from New England.

Moving back to the Midwest was good in one sense—my family was happier—but the challenges faced by the college were not any easier. Siena

Heights, too, had been a distinguished women's college until the 1960s, when dwindling enrollment convinced the trustees to begin accepting men. When I arrived in 1977, the college was coed in name only. There were few men on campus and fewer applicants. Something had to be done. After much observation, campus meetings and lots of thinking, I became convinced that we needed to add an athletic program to attract men. First up was basketball. The problem was there was no basketball court on campus. So, we did the next best thing—we used the elementary school gym at St. Joseph's Catholic School. This was okay except our players had to jog to and from the facility every day.

With no home court on which to play home games, we were forced to use the elementary school gym and all the spectators had to sit on the stage in order to cheer on the team. But, cheer they did. Siena Heights was blessed with a top rate Board of Trustees and a very caring faculty. The chair of the board, Chester Devenow, was an outstanding businessman and a true leader. One of the first things he asked me to do when I arrived was to make a recommendation concerning the construction of a field house.

After less than one week of study, I called Chester and said, "We should move ahead with all deliberate speed."

So, after raising another $600,000, we had the $1 million we needed to begin construction. Ten months later, we had our field house. The Siena spirit began developing and we began a winning tradition. We quickly added volleyball, track and field and cross-country.

I hired Pat Palmer as track coach and he began recruiting athletes from Ohio, where he had been before. Very quickly, our enrollment grew so that today, Siena Heights, now a university, has nearly 1,000 men and women on the Adrian campus plus another 1,200 to 1,300 on satellite campuses throughout the state of Michigan.

The field house had an immediate impact on the enrollment and on the public perception of the college by the community. In addition to adding soccer and tennis teams, we were able to focus attention on the college's strengths in art, music, science and teacher education. Additionally, we began an international education initiative and soon began attracting students from Asia, Latin America and Canada. However, the stark reality was that Siena Heights was endowment poor—with less than $1 million in the endowment and an enrollment of fewer than 800 students.

Creating a 'first-rate' university

Dr. James Ebben, vice president and provost at Siena Heights during Lou's tenure, is President Emeritus of Edgewood College where he served for 17 years as president. In the first half of his academic career, he was a philosophy professor, teaching mostly in small Catholic colleges. After about 17 years in the classroom and some funded research time, Ebben said, he served in various administrative positions such as academic dean, provost, academic vice president, interim president, and vice president of planning before becoming president of Edgewood College. His primary research interest is in "defining and maintaining institutional vitality in small colleges." Ebben retired from full-time college administration a few years ago. Besides family, which includes his wife Marilyn, three married children and nine grandchildren, international travel continues to be one of his primary interests. The Ebbens now call Madison, Wisconsin home.

"Lou and I are what seems like life-long colleagues and friends," Ebben said. "We first met about 35 years ago and worked together at Siena Heights College more than 30 years ago. Lou introduced me to his California family, mentored me in leadership in higher education, taught me many things about managing small colleges, traveled with me in China, and was always available for problem solving and just good conversation.

"In Father Hesburgh's foreword, he mentions Lou's extensive international work, especially in China, and Lou's interest in creating first-rate Catholic universities. Lou taught me long ago that these two things go together. Even before global thinking was widely promoted in academic and economic circles, Lou saw the educational value of bringing together different cultures on college campuses especially in small colleges where many students came from parochial backgrounds. 'Everyone wins,' he once told me, 'the capable and promising international students who might otherwise not have a chance at higher education, and the American students who are stimulated and challenged by interacting with students from other cultures.'"

Ebben, like Lou, sees the importance of international student exchanges.

"The international students who come to the American campuses help to raise the level of education by challenging both faculty and students," he said. "Bringing a sizable number of international students onto a college campus is one way to follow Father Hesburgh's prescription for building first-rate universities by 'attracting the right faculty and bright, promising students.'"

When Lou came to Siena Heights College in the late seventies, Ebben recalls, "I was in my second year at Siena Heights doing research funded by FIPSE on how to keep small colleges academically vital without having resources to continually hire new faculty.

"My research fit right into one of Lou's primary interests, which was that of building first rate Catholic universities."

At the end of the grant period, Ebben says, Lou hired him as academic dean and then provost of the college.

"Lou was a great mentor for me in these roles," Ebben says. "Many evenings, he invited me into his office after everyone else had left and we sipped a glass of wine together and discussed how we were doing in moving the college forward. It was in these meetings that Lou convinced me that I had the needed skills to be a college president.

"During our tenure together before he left Siena to take the presidency of The College of St Rose in Albany, New York, Lou and I and our families also developed a very close friendship. In good humor we called him 'flying Lou' after Bernard Slade's late sixties sitcom, 'The Flying Nun,' starring Sally Fields."

Ebben reflected again on Hesburgh's comments.

"He observed Lou's devotion to the ongoing work of assisting international students," Ebben said. "His flying off to faraway places was only to attract interesting students and others to come to his institution to provide stimulus to the academic environment. He strongly believed that new and fresh ideas were the life blood of any college campus, and any means of making that happen would improve the chances of creating an electrifying environment to promote learning."

Ebben pointed to Lou's fascination with the PBS series, "Meeting of the Minds," starring Steve Allen and his wife, Jayne Meadows. Actors portrayed famous people who had played significant roles in history. Guests would interact with each other and with Allen, who hosted the show, discussing philosophy, religion, history, science and many other topics.

"Lou said to me that this was exactly what should be happening on college campuses," Ebben remembered. "Then he asked, 'How about inviting Steve Allen and Jayne Meadows to campus? We can award them honorary degrees in recognition of their outstanding work.'"

The result was Siena's own "Meeting of Minds," featuring faculty members in the roles of famous people from history, literature, philosophy and religion.

"All of it created a vibrant atmosphere," Ebben said. "Steve Allen and Jayne Meadows were only two of the many interesting people who graced the campus of Siena Heights College during Lou's tenure."

Ebben calls Lou "very effective in making exciting things happen.

"I have heard many comment that there is never a dull moment when Lou is around," Ebben says. "This is true. Even though at times when working with Lou life would be hectic, you always knew that in the end progress would have been made toward his goal of building a first-rate university."

Within a few years, Siena had nearly 100 international students and a wholly different culture emerged. The school added six off-campus centers and its overall enrollment ballooned to 2,100 students.

During my tenure at Siena, I made my first trip to China using visas issued through Pakistan. At that time, U.S. citizens could not get visas to China; it was necessary to use a third party. It opened up a whole new chapter in my life. It was the first of 35 visits and I was able to develop many connections there as well as bring many Chinese students to Siena. Other international students also arrived from Venezuela, Peru, Brazil, Mexico and beyond.

From the beginning, convincing the faculty and especially the Dominican sisters this was the key to improving and sustaining Siena was not an easy sell—but it worked.

While I was at Siena, I started a tradition that I carried with me to the end of my professional career as a college president. In 1978, I cooked—with the help of students—a traditional Italian family dinner. Nearly 700 students and staff attended the first dinner. For me, it is just another way to show the students how much we care for them. In return, the international students were prompted to organize an annual "International Dinner" to express their appreciation.

All of this, of course, required a lot of energy and time and I am afraid it took a severe toll on my wife and children.

They never complained but I became aware that things were not all that great on the home front. Then, almost out of the blue, Jean informed me she wanted a divorce. I was stunned and devastated. It did not immediately occur to me at that time but it has since. I was not giving my wife and family the attention they needed and deserved.

And so, shortly after the Christmas of 1982, the inevitable occurred—our marriage fell apart.

Soon after, Jean left with Justin for California and I began interviewing for positions out east.

I had three offers, one in Florida and two in New York. I finally settled on the College of Saint Rose in Albany, New York since it was close to New Hampshire where Mary Lou and Terri lived.

It turned out to be a good move and it was the start of a slow healing and learning experience for me—more hard lessons were in store.

The College of Saint Rose

In August 1983, I returned east. I had signed an initial one-year contract for $59,000 to be president of The College of Saint Rose, where I would finish my formal academic career. This was a very difficult time for me because my marriage had fallen apart and I arrived in Albany knowing no one at St. Rose. Although Justin was with me for a time, he really wanted to be with his mom. Within a year, he left and went back to finish high school and I stayed at Saint Rose, where I quickly learned that some faculty and religious were not too thrilled to have a divorced Catholic as their new president.

Sometimes their disdain manifested itself in strange ways. Because the college had a deferred maintenance problem—approximately $10 million in needs—a lot needed doing and quickly.

The day I directed the maintenance crew to apply a coat of paint on an old building that housed the admissions office, I received a call from a couple of the sisters who complained I was "changing everything" by having the office exterior painted white instead of their beloved brown, one of the school colors. That was a portent of things to come.

For a few years, some of the faculty would complain they wanted more money, more parking and less emphasis on adding athletic programs (to attract more men).

Another major issue was my directive that we begin using "College of Saint Rose" instead of the "CSR" moniker recommended by a consultant. Some of the reasoning as to why we should use "CSR" was that good money had been spent for the advice. But a few semesters of using the full name of the college began to pay off. We began getting better media coverage, enrollments were climbing and the college began attracting a much wider range of students, especially from abroad. Enrollment slowly grew from 2,675 to 4,200 in the year I retired. Today, the overall enrollment exceeds 5,100. In retrospect, I believe our strategies were the correct ones. Today, Saint Rose is one of the premier colleges in the Capital Region of New York.

Rev. Christopher DeGiovine

Father Chris DeGiovine is dean of spiritual life and chaplain at The College of Saint Rose.

"I met Lou when I applied for the job of Chaplain at The College of Saint Rose where he was president. That was in 1990. We have been colleagues and friends ever since. Lou was always supportive of my work and ministry at the college. We were able to do great work to grow the institution while Lou was here.

"Lou is a man of many ideas and boundless energy. He is always coming up with new ideas to pursue and always was sending memos to his Cabinet to think about this or consider doing that or asking if we (I) had thought of doing this. He is committed to and genuinely loves his work.

"My favorite memory of Lou was the day we met to finalize the college plans for a new multicultural center on campus. Many strong voices were advocating the center focus on American minorities. Lou was adamant, clear and articulate in his advocacy for an intercultural, global understanding of minorities as the way to truly diversify the college and to bring about the greatest global awareness to our campus. His vision was right on and several years before its time."

Mary Grondahl

Mary Grondahl, vice president of The College of Saint Rose, has known Lou since 1983. When Lou arrived at Saint Rose, Mary was working in the school's admissions office.

"Lou had and still has an impressive global view of the world, long before it was fashionable to do so," Grondahl said. "His love and respect for the Chinese people and their country is magnificent."

She acknowledged that while Lou was its president, The College of Saint Rose enrolled the "largest and most diverse international student population in the college's history." This included many students from China and Turkey, the two countries from which the highest number of Saint Rose students were recruited.

"Lou tended to these global partnerships and to the students who enrolled as a result with detailed attention," Grondahl said. "He cared and still cares deeply about each student. He had an open door policy for students who needed help navigating the unfamiliar U.S. college system. Several of the students who enrolled at Saint Rose through these partnerships have become influential leaders in their fields and they are giving back to Saint Rose in productive ways.

"In a real sense, Lou's influence lives on through the alumni who came to Saint Rose because of him."

Grodahl said she considers "Lou's vision to further develop Saint Rose's enrollment and influence through athletics to be one of his crowning achievements.

"It continues to flourish even after his retirement," she said.

"Lou had the foresight to develop athletic teams so that the college could increase and diversify its enrollment and further develop brand perception of Saint Rose."

Grondahl said Lou's goals were to expand the school's geographic "footprint," as well as bring more male students to the campus and to align Saint Rose with other institutions that had higher brand awareness at that time than Saint Rose carried.

"Today, the College competes in the Northeast-10 Athletic Conference - one of the most - if not the most competitive NCAA Division II conferences in the country," Grondahl said. "More important, every time the College competes against Bentley, LeMoyne, St. Michael's, Merrimack, and Stonehill, for example, the Saint Rose brand perception is carried beyond the primary territory."

Grondahl praises Lou's ability to elevate the community's awareness and perception of The College of Saint Rose.

"He developed meaningful partnerships and relationships with the community and with government leaders," she explained. "His leadership and vision were the first step in paving the way for what has become three decades of sustained growth and development at Saint Rose. I often tell those with whom I meet that it was Lou Vaccaro who set the stage for the college's growth and rising brand perception in the wider community."

Grondahl calls Lou a "hands-on" president "who had a vision but also saw his role as an implementer.

"He could lead discussions with community and government leaders during the day and cook and serve spaghetti for guidance counselors at night," she commented. "He went to all of the basketball games and hosted student and other college groups in his home. Lou was a 'real world' leader for Saint Rose—he provided the vision and developed community spheres of influence. At the same time, he would roll up his sleeves to do what was necessary to advance the Saint Rose cause."

On a more personal note, Grondahl said she has "a remarkably rewarding career because Lou took a professional chance on me when the director of admissions position opened in 1986.

"He made me acting director and then accepted the recommendation of the search committee to make me director of admissions in the same year," Grondahl recalls. "Without his confidence, I cannot imagine I would have experienced such rich personal and professional successes. I am very grateful that he took that leap of faith in an untested professional— something that I can now say he did—and does often—in his life and work."

Welcoming Arkansas Governor Bill Clinton to The College of Saint Rose on the same day Clinton visited New York Governor Cuomo, seeking his support during this primary swing through New York. Gov. Clinton's wife, Hilary Clinton, spoke to an overflow gathering on campus.

Lou in 1980 at Siena Heights

Siena Soccer Club in 1979.

Chapter 11
A Fresh Start

While at Saint Rose, I had the opportunity to make new friends, many of whom were like me, single parents who were divorced or widowed. I met many nice, young, unmarried women. Many of them were divorced and I was invited to a variety of social events. Of course, I accepted and was appreciative of that. One day, one of the deans came by my office and asked what I was doing after work that evening. He suggested I join him for a wine and cheese event at the college that was being hosted for the supervisors of our college teachers. There would be a lot of teachers there, he said, and it might be a nice change of pace for me. And sure enough there were about 40-50 women there, ranging in age from 28 to 68. I went around thanking them for the help they had given to the college in educating and training prospective teachers for the various school districts in our area. The last woman I met was Linda Lasher, who was not too thrilled to be there. I discovered she'd been widowed and was a single mother. Her son was finishing high school and, in fact, she told me that her son was coming to the college the following weekend to try out for the jazz band because he was an accomplished musician. So, I gave her my card and told her that I'd be happy to help him out in any way possible. She promptly put the card in her pocket and that was the end of my evening. The next day, after thinking about all the people I'd met, I decided to call Linda. I was able to get her name and phone number from the Admissions Office since her son was coming to campus and I called a couple of evenings later and introduced myself. She was very pleasant on the phone and I asked how her son was doing. She said that he did enjoy the tryout with the band but wasn't sure if he would end up at St. Rose or Colgate. He also had received a congressional appointment to West Point. I said, "Well let me know if there's something I can do for you, it sounds like he's a good student." I promptly began talking about other opportunities we might participate in together.

First, I asked her to join me for lunch but she refused because she said she was seeing someone at the time. I asked if it would be okay if I called her from time to time to see how things were going. As it turned out, I called her every evening for a month and at the end of that time she admitted she wasn't actually seeing anyone. Finally, she agreed to visit my home where my daughter Michelle was living at the time. We had an evening of good conversation. I found her to be an excellent conversationalist although she still was grieving the loss of her husband. We became good friends. We would talk every night and sometimes she would join me for college events. Her son, Jim, and my daughter, Michelle, often accompanied us. This went on for three or four years. We would see each other frequently. Linda was a big help to me when I had to entertain visitors at the president's home and she was a good listener. That's what I needed at the time. She did a lot for me and in 1984, when I went to China, she would check on the house, make sure the mail was picked up and generally keep an eye on things for me, all the while teaching middle school in nearby Colonie, New York. After four and a half years of being close friends, talk of marriage came up. I kiddingly tell people I accepted her proposal.

We chose my birthday—July 25—so I would never forget the date of our marriage and we were wed in 1987, four years after I arrived in Albany from Adrian. During the time at Saint Rose, and especially after I got married, I would travel to China every year, teach and lecture there and bring students back. Linda later became involved and was able to come with me on four different occasions. The young students loved her, knowing she was a teacher, but she also was a good conversationalist and fine ambassador for the United States. We did a number of things together at the college and were able to host students not only from China and Japan but also from Poland. Linda took it upon herself to develop a special educational exchange program with students from Poland that lasted the good part of a summer.

I spent 14 years at St. Rose and during that time, it was transformed to a full-blown co-ed school with athletic and graduate programs. Enrollment went from 3,200 students to 4,600 students and the brand was established by the time I retired. We welcomed international students from 30 countries, including Turkey, China, Japan, Korea, Brazil and Mexico. Linda retired in 1995 and I retired in 1996. I continued to maintain ties internationally and returned to China on numerous occasions. I continued to write and publish but I was getting tired. Linda and I began thinking about where we were going to live in our retirement. Florida and Virginia were considered and then vetoed because the summers were hot and humid. We tried California, but it was just too expensive. So, we settled on Las Vegas, where we live during the winter months.

Lou at Red Rock Canyon near Las Vegas with Ms. Wang Bei, CEO of Shanghai Skyway General Aviation Company, Mr. Zou Jianming, President of Shanghai Zenisun Investment Company, Mr. Zhang Baokong, General Manager of Shanghai Skyway General Aviation Company and Mr. Wu Zhendong, CEO of Hongkong Avion Pacific limited Company.

Daniel Tan, post-graduate student at The College of Saint Rose, currently resides in Shanghai, China.

Chapter 12
International Impact

While I was at Marycrest and St. Ambrose, I met a young professor of philosophy from Nigeria. Chris Nwodo had just finished his doctorate in philosophy on Heidigger. We became close friends. One day, Chris called me and said, "Louie, I know you have a great interest in international students. Can you help me by creating some scholarships so I can bring Nigerian students to the U.S.?"

It was an intriguing idea. Chris told me, "you don't need money—you just create a special scholarship or a discounted tuition program for them." We began doing this and soon Marycrest became so popular, students were coming in who didn't need scholarships.

I used to argue incessantly with faculty and staff that we weren't giving money away, we were doing just the opposite because international students were producing additional revenues. Eventually we brought in more than 300 Chinese students and several hundred others from other countries through this type of arrangement.

The real benefit in bringing these international students in was to raise the level of intellectual diversity that previously wasn't found in many of these institutions. We also sent faculty abroad and they would return much more culturally aware. It really helped build the enrollment base at schools like Marycrest, Siena and Saint Rose.

I liked the challenge of building these kinds of programs and I liked being able to bring students from around the world into the U.S. It really was a win-win for everyone.

Lou's experiences with international students shaped his career as a college president. He brought his work ethic and expertise with people to bear on building his relationships with people across the globe.

The lives of hundreds of international students have been changed as a result of their paths intersecting with Lou's educational philosophy. True to his word, he was able to help them achieve their dreams in ways they could not have imagined. Each has a special story to tell about how their lives were changed through their encounters with "Dr. Lou."

Joao Jose "JJ" Werzbitzki

JJ Werzbitzki resides in Curitiba, Brazil, where he makes great use of the education he received from Siena Heights College, now Siena Heights University. A retired university professor—he taught advertising and public relations—JJ still works as a marketing communications consultant, is writing a book about modern advertising, "Publicitar," and doing some work as a blogger. Find him at http//:blogs.abril.com.br/blogdojj, JJ's Blog. About 9,000 people read him each day.

"I first met Dr. Lou Vaccaro at Siena Heights College in 1978 when I arrived there with a scholarship for journalism from the Rotary Foundation.

"Dr. Vaccaro was always a great teacher and friend and helped me to transform my specialization in journalism into a master's degree in arts and communications, with a lot of work, study and encouragement. Always, even when I had some difficulties with English or with my classes, Dr. Vaccaro was a help to me.

"Dr. Vaccaro loves Brazil and soccer and I was glad that I was able to help him by being part of the Siena Heights Saints Soccer Team. We had some victories and a lot of fun. We had a great season in 1978-79.

"I remember when in our first game, we beat Toledo University (now The University of Toledo). Dr. Vaccaro was so excited that he threw us an enormous party on campus.

"Dr. Vaccaro was very important in my life. First of all, he became my Rotary tutor in Adrian when my first tutor wasn't taking appropriate care of me. Dr. Vaccaro helped with all my personal and student needs and gave me the opportunity to work in the College's Public Relations department. I had previous experience with that in Brazil before coming to the U.S.

"We traveled to Detroit for interviews and talked a lot about my future, my scholarship, my studies and my life at Siena. After five or six months in Adrian, I came back to Brazil and married Eliane and we both came back to Siena, where she was able to do some advanced studies in Special Education, again thanks to Dr. Vaccaro's help.

"When we arrived at Siena, Dr. Vaccaro organized a party with some friends to welcome Eliane and also gave us a guest room at Siena, which provided us with lots of comfort and privacy. It was a great honeymoon!

"We had all the happiness that we could have imagined as 'just married' students and being a friend of Dr. Vaccaro during our time at Siena. It was a wonderful and unforgettable time.

"One time, Dr. Vaccaro invited Eliane and I to an Easter Dinner, featuring a wonderful and enormous turkey and a very friendly reception from Dr. Vaccaro's wife, Jean, and son, Justin.

"After we left Siena in 1979, I lost contact with Dr. Vaccaro.

"Some years ago, I tried to find him on a site from China but I was unable to make contact with him. Then in June 2010, I found him through the Internet and we were able to reconnect.

"Dr. Vaccaro is a very kind person. He is dedicated, professional, ethical and a great friend. He is one of the people responsible for my professional development in advertising, public relations and journalism.

"Dr. Vaccaro gave me the power to grow in a different country, with a different language, but with the understanding of true friendship, counseling and help.

"Eliane and I will always be grateful for Dr. Vaccaro's friendship."

Iqbal Roshd

Iqbal Roshd is now a successful businessman in Toronto, where he owns a number of Tim Hortons franchises. He graduated from Siena Heights in 1982 with a degree in business. In 2007, he was among the outstanding alumni honored.

"I was fortunate enough to meet Dr. Vaccaro 32 years ago. In the summer and fall of 1978, I had written to some 31 different universities and colleges and received six scholarships. The late Sister Anne Marie Brown was the director of admissions at Siena at that time. She offered me a partial scholarship and a very encouraging letter. Upon acceptance, there was a letter from the college president, who, at that time, was Dr. Vaccaro. I found that very impressive. I didn't know any school president that was sending invitation letters to incoming freshmen. My parents were very impressed. So, we all decided that I would attend Siena. Plus, Michigan is much closer to Montreal than some of the other places I had applied to, including Iowa, Texas, Kansas and Kentucky. That was the beginning of my Siena Heights journey. Little did I know that my life would take a big turn for the better."

Daniel Tan

Daniel Tan, who later became one of Lou's good friends, comments on his friendship. Daniel Tan came to the College of Saint Rose while Lou was president there. He had been a teacher and school principal in China before spending a year as an "exchange student" at the college.

"I used to think university presidents were knowledgeable but inaccessible, due to their busy and rigorous lives. I changed my mind when I met Dr. Lou Vaccaro, who is an easy-going and very approachable man.

"In my experience, Dr. Vaccaro was always concerned about the school, its administrative staff, its faculty and its students. He considers himself a teacher who is mission-bound to give others guidance and instruction, a friend who is always ready to help people with any problems they encountered.

"Although he was busy with academic affairs, Dr. Vaccaro met and talked to everyone. He ate with students in the cafeteria and went to basketball games to cheer on the school team. He would attend student parties and other events because he enjoyed spending his time with students and staff.

"The Chinese students hold Dr. Vaccaro in the highest regard. He is considered a knowledgeable teacher and friendly man who can always find a solution to any problems they had.

"Dr. Vaccaro has a pioneering spirit. When he became president of The College of Saint Rose, he adopted a strategic approach to increasing the enrollment at the school by adding a large number of international students, targeting developing countries like my native China. He traveled a lot and everywhere he went, he was an ambassador for Saint Rose.

Through his efforts, the college formed sister-school ties with Jilin Normal University in China for an exchange program and signed an agreement with the Shu Ping Scholarship Foundation for two Chinese students to attend Saint Rose each year. The number of foreign students rose from almost zero when he took office to more than 100 at its peak, representing a significant increase in the total enrollment.

"I was curious about what the office of an American university president would look like. The office was tidy and the walls filled with framed photographs and memorabilia. My eyes were drawn to Dr. Vaccaro's father's plumbing license, which was framed and in a place of prominence. I asked him why he had his father's plumbing license on the wall and he told me that it was to remind him that his parents had a humble background and he should not forget the hardships and sufferings he and his family had gone through.

"He told me that a person can't change their family background but a person can change his future through his own efforts. If a person wants to be successful, he needs to work hard and be persistent.

"In the United States, there does not seem to be a prejudice against a person's background. A successful man with a humble origin is a man who is capable and wise. This is a man who has overcome many obstacles through persistent hard work. Dr. Vaccaro's humble family background has motivated him to continue to achieve success.

"Dr. Vaccaro has visited China many times and has said he was impressed by the hospitality of the Chinese people and the diligence of Chinese students. He has always cherished his friendship with the Chinese.

"When I was a student at the College of Saint Rose, Dr. Vaccaro helped me find work in the computer lab. This was beneficial because I learned a lot about computers and improved my computer skills.

"Dr. Vaccaro and his wife, Linda, often pick up international students from the Albany airport and if they do not have a place to stay right away, the Vaccaros arranged for the students to stay with them until school accommodations were ready. They also invited the Chinese students to dinner frequently so that Chinese students could experience American culture and the American lifestyle. Before a Chinese student left for home, the Vaccaros would prepare a care package with food and toiletries to get them started. It warmed all our hearts and left a deep, unforgettable impression.

"The first Christmas after I left the U.S., I received a beautiful Christmas card from the Vaccaros. Dr. Vaccaro had added to his signature a stamp with a Chinese seal that featured the Chinese version of his name. I will never forget the time I spent in the U.S."

Musun "David" Li

Musun "David" Li, a long-time friend and associate of Lou's recalls the many lives Lou touched throughout his professional career. "Li Musun is one of my dearest friends," Lou says, "He is a week older than I am and his son came to Saint Rose to study. Li says that his son is a Christian and his wife is a Christian but he is not a Christian. Yet, Lou claims that David is the most Christian man he's met in his entire life. He has done so much for people—he's brought a lot of Chinese students to the U.S. through grant programs."

"Jades are usually enclosed in hard rock shells. In many cases, so are talents. Both need keen, penetrating and experienced eyes to find them out. Dr. Vaccaro has a pair of such eagle's keen eyes.

"When my nephews Maurice and Jacob Chi first came to the States, they knew not more than a dozen English words. How were they admitted as students of Siena Heights University? How did Dr. Vaccaro break through the shell?

"Dr. Vaccaro always loves to tell people that when Jacob and Maurice first came over, they knew not more than a dozen English words. But, Jacob is now a well-known professor at Colorado State University and the conductor of the Pueblo Symphony Orchestra. Maurice is a very successful IT executive with Thompson-Reuters in Boston.

"Dr. Vaccaro and I are buddy-buddies, joking with each other. I called myself CIA—Chinese in America—and he called himself FBI—full-blooded Italian. I am nine days older yet he is much taller. Our friendship comes from a shared belief in helping people. In 1988, he helped set up the J.L. Koo Scholarship at the College of Saint Rose. In the year 2000, he helped me obtain a grant of $300,000 from the Freeman Foundation. With that, I sent over to the U.S. some 15 graduate students, helped more than 6,000 jobless persons in China and bought a house to serve as an assembly place for young entrepreneurs.

"Wang Hui was a Koo Scholarship student at the College of Saint Rose, in the early 1990s. During his first year, his English was really poor. I was in charge of the scholarship. Dr. V. had to write to me and together we issued a warning to Wang Hui, saying if he did not improve his English, he would be sent back to China; this almost scared him to death, but, he managed to pass his classes. He is now a successful physician in Tacoma, Washington, licensed for both Western and traditional Chinese medicine. Some students are smart and quick-minded; some are slow but very persistent. Lou can always find the right way to deal with them.

"I have learned a lot from Dr. Vaccaro: the Christian spirit of sharing and helping. He has sent several hundred students from China to this country, many with scholarships, and is still working hard for the Sino-American friendship today.

"The Chi and Li families are booming in the States. What we have earned from society should be returned to society.

"In human society, we have to set up general regulations and rules but there are always exceptions. Clever dealing with the exceptions beyond the general rule will lead to victory. This was discussed by Sun Tzu in his famous *Art of War*. Lou proved him to be a good leader and could make good use of his authority. Bole was a very famous, legendary man in Chinese history. It was said that he had the ability to find the fastest steed from ordinary horses even the steed appeared in bad shape. A famous Chinese writer said if you do not treat the steed like a steed but like an ordinary work horse, hard work and bad food will shatter the steed and it will die someday in the farmer's stable. His conclusion is: "No Bole, no best steed," and I'd say "no Lou Vaccaro, no success of many international students.""

Elizabeth Wang

Elizabeth Wang has known Lou for sixteen years.

"The first time I met Dr. Vaccaro was at his office at The College of Saint Rose. It was the beginning of the fall semester in 1994, and I was a new arrival from China in the international student program. An assistant brought me to Dr. Vaccaro's office. He was standing there behind the desk putting something down. I was a little nervous but very excited because it was the first time in my life I would be meeting a college president. Dr. Vaccaro welcomed me with his big smile and a handshake. I remember it clearly even sixteen years later.

"A few months later, I met him again at a Chinese New Year party in early 1995. But rather than talking about school, news or studying, we talked about food. At the party, each of the Chinese students was asked to make at least one dish to pass around. I brought

Sweet and Sour Sliced Potatoes. It is not the kind of food you would get in a Chinese restaurant, it's more of the simple staple kind of dish you'd eat at home.

"Dr. Vaccaro attended the party and he sampled all the food the Chinese students made. I noticed Dr. Vaccaro went back to get a second helping of Sour and Sweet Sliced Potatoes a few times. We started to talk. We discussed how to make Sour and Sweet Sliced Potatoes and which part of China the dish is commonly found. We also talked about the cooking and eating culture in China. I still remember that party and the visit with Dr. Vaccaro. It was the first time I could appreciate that cooking could contribute so much to social life. I was so happy to find out the dish I made was enjoyed by so many people from so many different cultures. It has become my specialty since then. I now make this dish often as a treat to my international friends.

"People can be influenced or changed by many things, big or small. Dr. Vaccaro was one of those influences in my life, a person who impacted me, sometimes by just a single word.

"I remember a talk I had with Dr. Vaccaro in 2009. I shared with him that I had volunteered to teach at an elementary school at a very poor mountain village in southwest China in 2007. Dr. Vaccaro shared his experience on a trip helping children from poor families in China. He said the kids there were wonderful and beautiful and he was so impressed by their smiles. He said they were happy children, despite their hardships.

"The word "happy" really made me rethink my teaching career. I was so focused on making sure the students were gaining knowledge that I ignored the most important part of their learning—to find their wonderful nature and be proud of who they are. Dr. Vaccaro showed me that help isn't just what you offer to others but what you can find out from them.

"As one of his students, I always felt Dr. Vaccaro has the kind of personality that makes people around him feel relaxed and encouraged. He is able to lift any barrier between people, whether language, culture or anything else."

Maria Miroshnichenko-Jarosh

Maria Miroshnichenko-Jarosh is a former English professor and former head of the Foreign Languages Department at Vasyl Stefanyk Precarpathian National University, Ivano-Frankivsk, Ukraine.

"My husband Bohdan (Dan) Jarosh and I met Louis Vaccaro in 1998, when my son Alex entered the bachelor's degree program at Trinity College in Vermont. Our relationship with Dr. Vaccaro became very warm and pleasant from the very beginning. It was amazing that Dr. Vaccaro could find time for all the international students at Trinity College and their parents, whenever they came to visit their children and, above and beyond that, to take care of all of the students at all times, in addition to performing his other essential responsibilities as college president.

"With his professionalism, kindness, care, and support, Dr. Vaccaro became a model of an American professor for our family. My son's stories about his life at the college were often connected with the name of Professor Louis Vaccaro, who contributed to his progress, and provided a great example of the leadership and support that guided Alex on the path of success in his studies. With Dr. Vaccaro's wise guidance and advice, Alex succeeded to be placed on the Dean's list of the distinguished students at both colleges he attended. Of course, our family truly appreciated Dr. Vaccaro's support and assistance, and my late husband used to say "'I wish I could have had such a president at my College." When I invited Dr. Vaccaro to visit our house in Saratoga Springs, while on his way to Albany, Dan said he was sure the professor would not have any time for us, but Dr. Vaccaro found the time to visit us, he really enjoyed our famous Ukrainian food, including pierogies, and we were delighted to receive him as an honored guest at our place. One could only imagine how pleased we were to listen to the stories about the College life in general and my son's studies in particular. Dr. Vaccaro continued supporting my son and he later recommended Alex to transfer to Siena Heights University in Adrian, Michigan. He believed such a transfer would be beneficial for Alex to learn the culture and the American way of life. Today Alex is an MBA graduate from the State University of New York in Albany and he continues to seek advice from Dr. Vaccaro, while leading his consulting ventures around the world.

"When Louis learned that I used to teach at the Precarpathian National University in Ukraine, he offered me an opportunity to assist him in recruiting new students from Ukraine. The task was almost unattainable, due to the standard of living in the former Soviet Union countries as compared to that of the western nations. That difference usually made it impossible for the local students to afford interna- tional studies. However, when Dr. Vaccaro became Georgian Court College president in Lakewood, N.J., I was actually able to attract one student from Ukraine. As with my son Alex, I was certain that she would be in good hands as a new international student at the college.

We have always had a terrific time when we had a chance to get together with Louis and his wonderful wife Linda. Linda is a retired schoolteacher, a very well educated, intelligent and charming woman. Louis is a real expert in education matters, very wise, knowl- edgeable and a charismatic person. Therefore, we quickly found common topics to discuss with both of them. Our conversations were filled with riveting discussions ranging from politics to education, to the way of life in America and overseas. The Vaccaros have always been very attentive and wise partners in discussions, the advice they offered was that of smart people who are knowledgeable and open-minded, able to understand the concerns and interests of their audience.

"Both Dr.Vaccaro and his wife Linda were of great support for us in 2000, when my husband died of a heart attack. It was Louis' advice that brought me to work as an English as a Second Language Professor at Aurora College in Shanghai, China, for 5 years. An Honorable Professor at Aurora College, he has many devoted friends and colleagues at the University, as well as throughout China. 'A new philosophy of life and my friends in Shanghai will help you recover from your despair and depression, Maria,' Dr. Vaccaro told me. 'Your expertise will help the students at Aurora succeed in their English studies.' It should be mentioned that Louis didn't simply recommend me to move to Shanghai. He personally took the time to write a recommendation letter for me and called his colleagues in Shanghai to ensure that this transition went as smoothly as possible. He always took the time to visit Aurora College, attend my classes and meet my students, whenever he was able while traveling on business to China. And, yes, Dr. Vaccaro was correct as usual—my new friends and colleagues and a different lifestyle in China had indeed helped me to recover from my sorrows and to begin enjoying my life and especially my teaching career again. Besides, in China, I had the honor of meeting many wonderful people and making a lot of great friends. I still keep in touch with my students from Aurora College and my Chinese friends via phone and email.

"The Vaccaro family's wise guidance and advice to my daughter Alisa and her then- fiancé Alex was crucial at a time when they had just moved to the United States from Ukraine in 2001. Louis and Linda were honorable guests at their wedding ceremony in July 2002.

"Both Louis and Linda's kind support and advice helped Alisa and Alex to adjust to the new culture and lifestyle in the United States. They have succeeded, and ultimately became successful in their life here and careers as an accountant for the New York State agency and a systems engineer for the IT consulting company respectively.

"I was very impressed to have found out that Dr. Vaccaro is deeply respected and admired by his students across the world, including China. His Chinese students call him their Godfather. Today, I am certain that he has become an unofficial Godfather for my family as well.

"My family has come to deeply appreciate the Vaccaros' friendship, wisdom and support during the years we have known them. It is really a blessing to have met such wonderful, professional, brilliant, respectable, and at the same time gracious and humble people. We consider it to be our true honor to be able to call them friends."

Maurice Chi

Maurice Chi and his family have known Lou for more than 30 years, having first met when Maurice was a student at Siena Heights in the late 1970s.

I regard Dr. Vaccaro as a facilitator, educator, good person, dear friend, great mentor and, above all, a loving father. Lao Zi (Lao Tsu) said in his "Dao De Jing" that the greatest goodness is water. Dr. Vaccaro is just like water. He is a good man. I am using the simplest adjective --good' --to describe him, but simple holds the key. Water is simple, but it forms and supports life. Water is goodness. Goodness is the universal virtue that's immutable from a subjective aspect in which it varies from individual to individual, from place to place, and from time to time. Dr.

Vaccaro is the goodness that needs not be proven good. Once you let him touch your life, his goodness flows within you and between you.

Dr. Vaccaro started working as a newspaper boy when he was very young. He wanted to be a teacher, so he worked very hard and saved every penny to pursue his education. His personal history reminded me of many new immigrants including my own--- financially poor yet spiritually rich. He had an alternative to poverty and that alternative is the pursuit of happiness in education. A man enjoys life after his education. A good man extends his education to others by providing opportunities. Dr. Vaccaro has done just that and Dr. Vaccaro is a good man.

Dr. Vaccaro is also my role model--humble and modest. He has helped hundreds of international students to study in the U.S. and build their successful American dreams. But he always speaks about how successful his students are--never once have I heard him talking about his own success. However, his words are always inspiring, witty and, sometimes, quite humorous. When he was the president at Siena Heights College, he invited all of the foreign students to his house on Columbus Day for dinner. Watching us wondering about his residence, he said, "Did you know Columbus was an Italian?" It may have sounded as though he were bragging about his Italian roots. But it was inspirational to the international student body that the people who have made a successful living in American were at one time foreigners. If you are as determined as Columbus was to be successful, you will be successful.

He always shares his fatherly advice with students. I, for one, was lucky to be a constant recipient.

In the movie, "The Godfather," the Godfather declares, "I take care of my family." Once Dr. Vaccaro knows you, you will always be a member of his family.

Lilia Roman

Lilia Roman lives in San Francisco but travels to Mexico frequently. One of twelve children from a very poor family in Mexico, she earned her degree in media and public communications, graduating with honors from The College of Saint Rose. After graduation, she traveled to South Korea, where she spent nine months teaching and traveling throughout Asia. When she returned to the U.S., she worked for a publishing company then went to Europe to learn French. About seven years ago, she started a company with three other people where she stayed for three years. Since leaving that company behind, she has been working for an engineering company helping with grant writing, research, translations, and other duties. She recently started a non-profit company with her sister in Mexico. They have helped fund several co-ops within the indigenous population of Morelos, Mexico, so people learn about self- sustainable development. Their goal is to create an organization in Mexico to keep funding social projects, teach people spiritual practices, educate people on the issues of the earth and the environment, and provide scholarships for disadvantaged children. The goal, says Lilia, is to launch the project yet this year.

"I've known Dr. Vaccaro for about 19 years. I first got acquainted with him over the phone as I was trying to help my older brother get an appointment with him. At the time, Dr. Vaccaro was president of The College of Saint Rose and my brother had been awarded a scholarship for undergraduate study. Dr. Vaccaro asked me about my own personal goals, whether I was in college and what I wanted to do. At the time, I was living in Washington, D.C. and attending a community college. I had been studying part-time, taking a few credits each semester and I couldn't see the end of my studies. I was also working full-time, and since things were not getting any easier for me, I wasn't sure whether I'd stay in the U.S. or return to Mexico, where I'm from. I was 22 years old when I first talked to Dr. Vaccaro.

"Soon he offered me a scholarship to the College of Saint Rose. I would only have to pay my living expenses. I accepted. Talking to him on the phone, he sounded more like a friend than a person I had not yet met in person. I felt like he really understood my struggles and my dreams and he just wanted to help. His voice was calming, confident, and reassuring, so much so that when I got off the phone, I had a lot more confidence in my future and what I was supposed to do here.

"Within a year, I was a Saint Rose student. It was such a blessing. When I met Dr. Vaccaro, I thought he was an angel. I was really taken by his strong but sensitive manner, by his professionalism, and by the way he seemed to be in control of all around him. He really wanted to give a voice to those that found it difficult to find one, and through his wisdom, he knew that transforming a human being helped transform the world. This is what really struck me about him: he inspired me to believe in humanity and the world again.

"That first year, I still wasn't quite sure about what I wanted to study but I had much energy, many hopes and a lot of dreams. Saint Rose gave me the tools I needed to find my path. Dr. Vaccaro was always encouraging and took the time to say "hello" to all of the international students and find out how we were doing. Whenever I met him on campus, he'd ask me how things were going; there was a continued communication with him and our international student group grew with the years.

"If I had to say one thing about how my experience with Dr. Vaccaro impacted my life, it is that he made me a stronger person who understood humility and he made me believe in myself, that I could do anything I wanted in this life. Most of all, I guess my experience with Dr. Vaccaro taught me never to give up on anything or anyone, much less myself. He taught more through his actions than through words. I can never thank him enough for all he gave me. I can only hope we gave him something valuable in return."

Zhou "Mimi" Mi

Zhou "Mimi" Mi earned a doctorate in management from the University of Science and Technology in China, located in Heifei in 2008, where she makes her home. She holds master's degrees in IT and management from the United Kingdom and hails from the Sichuan province of China. "Mimi" is married and the mother of a 6-year-old boy. She currently is the assistant to the president of international programs at U.S.T.C. and a faculty member at the school.

"I first met Dr. Vaccaro five years ago during a lecture he gave to the School of Management at the University of Science and Technology in China. He is a humorous man, warm-hearted, obliging and indefatigable. In 2007, he encouraged me to write a paper for an international conference. At that time, I didn't even know how to write a proper academic paper. He outlined the structure of the paper and instructed me to find relevant information, and then write the paper. Eventually, the paper was accepted by the conference and we were selected as the keynote speakers for the conference. Since then, I have co-authored five papers with him, all of which were accepted by various international conferences and indexed by EI or ISTP.

He is an easy person to get to know and to be friends with. He also is a wise elder, a helpful supervisor and a kind friend. I always found he had great suggestions for me, no matter what the issues. I consider myself fortunate to have such a great and wise friend."

Robert Lai

Robert Lai has known Lou more than 20 years. Robert and his wife, Rachel Liu live in Cleveland, Ohio, where Robert works for Tekino Corp. and his wife is on a three-year assignment with the Eaton Corporation. The couple has a daughter at Yale, Linda Lai and a son, Justin Lai, who is a freshman at Beechwood High School. He came to The College of Saint Rose to earn his Master's degree in Business Administration. He now is a consultant for a company that provides incubation services for business startups around the globe.

"When I first went to The College of Saint Rose in 1990, I was introduced to Professor Natalie Feinder by a friend who had studied at Columbia. Professor Feinder felt I would be comfortable at Saint Rose. When I discussed tuition, I was told I would pay the full amount, but at the end of the first semester, when I registered for the second semester, the registrar informed me I only owed half of the tuition. I was confused. I knew Dr. Vaccaro would often get a tuition waiver or computer lab job or a discount for Chinese students. Still I called him up and asked him if he paid for part of my tuition and he said yes. He helped me in a way that was very moving.

"In those days, most Chinese students came to study in the U.S. with very little money and they struggled financially. Dr. Vaccaro was kind and thoughtful and looked for ways to help. One day, he asked me if I would like him to introduce me to a banker he knew at Key Bank. I said, of course. So he introduced me to the senior vice president in charge of the international division and we sat at a table for lunch together. He asked me what he could do for me. I asked him for an internship. The banker asked if I was willing to work without pay and I agreed.

"Later, I asked Dr. Vaccaro why he had done that. He said, "Robert, I looked at your resume and I felt you could work there. You have great potential."

"In the summer of 1990, I got the internship with Key Bank and worked in the international area with human resources, operations and marketing. It was a very helpful experience. After two months as an intern, I was offered a part-time job. It helped support my studies. I was very grateful to Dr. Vaccaro because he had the ability to identify my strengths and place me in exactly the right kind of job. By doing this, he encouraged me to grow and have opportunities.

"After a few years, Dr. Vaccaro kept traveling to China and I worked for Key Bank and then later moved to First Union Bank in Washington, D.C. I would meet Lou frequently and once I told him how grateful I was for his support and encouragement. I asked him how I could repay him. He said, "Robert, you know you should keep the snowball rolling and treat others the way I treated you." He wanted me to help other Chinese students.

"So during the academic year, I would help students coming from China. Sometimes, Dr. Vaccaro could host them for a while—many of them came here with nothing but the clothes on their backs. When these students left his home, he would give them a gift. He still does that today; he gives his guests a little gift. It is an Italian custom as well as a Chinese custom.

"When he was president at Saint Rose, the college gave him a car to drive to and from school. But sometimes he would just walk to campus. If he happened to drive to campus, he would spend some time walking around and sometimes he would invite us to walk with him. He would greet every person, ask them how they were doing. He was nice to everyone. He knew what he was going to do every day to improve the school.

"Students knew they could come to Dr. Vaccaro's office anytime with a problem and he would address it immediately.

"I would estimate he helped more than 500 international students throughout his career.

"He is a humble man."

Steven Zhang

Steven Zhang calls Shanghai home but currently is studying at Dominican University of California. He has 15 years of working experience in Guangzhou, Hong Kong and Shanghai. Three of the 10 years he spent there involved working with American executive search firms, Manpower, MRI and Korn/Ferry International. All three of these companies are based in China.

"I was introduced to Dr. Vaccaro by an English teacher of mine when I expressed a desire to study in the United States in early 2010. Dr.Vaccaro immediately started to provide me with a great amount of information on choosing the right school, including an academic major that would benefit me and a location I would find favorable. In order for me to have a better understanding on the challenges and outcomes during a course of overseas studies, Dr. Vaccaro also has introduced me to two other Chinese students who had successfully studied in the U.S. under Dr. Vaccaro's guidance only a couple of years before.

"One of the students, who is currently working for the 2010 Shanghai World Expo shared with me the cultural differences between China and the U.S. and how much she enjoyed campus life in the States. She also shared with me her interesting traveling experience in South America. Another student who is running his own company in Shanghai talked with me about what I planned to do with overseas study. This student had gone to the States for his overseas studies at the age of 36. As I am also 36 now, his experience has become a very important endorsement of my traveling to the U.S."

"These two "senior" students have directly received Dr. Vaccaro's support during their overseas studies. They speak highly of his professionalism, generosity, sincerity and his great influence and encouragement with young people.

"Every time I have called him, he has been patient in answering my questions, even though the time difference between East and West might have caused a bit of inconvenience for him. His guidance and encouragement have been a big part of my success here. He will continue to be a mentor to me in all aspects of my life, studies and future career."

Presenting Governor Ronald Reagan with a book at Colby-Sawyer College while he was in New Hampshire for the first primary, 1975.

Zhou "Mimi" Mi,
Ph.D., is the assistant
to the president of
USTC in Hefei, China.

Mary Lou Yan (1)
and another student
with Lou at USTC,
2003.

Lou with his MBA students from the USTC at the
Higher Education forum in Hefei in 2002.

Chapter 13
The Classroom of Life

In addition to the formal learning I experienced through many mentors and teachers, there were innumerable unplanned and accidental hard lessons that resulted from my life as the grandson of an Italian stonemason and peasant homemaker who immigrated to the United States long before I was born. My parents were remarkable and taught their children many important lessons. Papa had many quaint but wise sayings that I continue to recall even in my eighth decade.

- There is only one kind of work that is no good—dishonest work!
- You are no better than anyone else—but neither are you worse.
- Anyone can be bad but it takes someone special to be good.
- You never can tell the depth of the well by the length of the handle on the pump.
- If you agree to do something—do it right the first time.
- God does not send a family another mouth to feed without sending another loaf of bread.
- Choose to work with your mind and not just your back.

- Watch your nickels and dimes, the dollars will take care of themselves.

  Mama's lessons were not as strident, but wise all the same, many delivered through her life and the example she set for us. For example, she believed one should never throw away a piece of bread without kissing the bread first and then tossing it only to the birds outside.

➢ Always a faithful church-goer, Mama was a lifelong member of her church choir—she took seriously St. Augustine's observation that "singing is praying twice."

➢ No one was ever turned away from our family's table—there was always enough food to add another two or three or four guests—invited or not!

➢ Not an outwardly affectionate person, Mama was always ready to extend a helping hand—even to strangers.

➢ And one of her constant admonitions was: "Don't argue with Papa, just do what he tells you!"

Of course, Little Nonna added her old country lessons as well—most often in Italian.

Additional lessons were provided by the scores of relatives in my life, including Uncle Minnie and Uncle Edward, Uncle Mike Vaccaro, Aunt Angeline and Aunt Jeannette and her husband, Uncle Pat Lynch, a.k.a. "Big Paddy;" Aunt Nellie Kelly and her husband, Uncle Bob Kelly. Most of their lessons were unplanned but all wisely delivered and with the best of intentions. Many of the lessons I picked up along the way resulted from my daily interaction with my five brothers and sister, "Virgie." Whether or not they learned anything from me remains up for debate. But there is no question the Vaccaro family was one big classroom.

Maurice Chi was one of the first international students to graduate from Siena Heights.
Photo by Dr. Robert Gordon

Pulitzer Prize author William Kennedy (l) with his wife, Dana, join Linda and Lou Vaccaro at a black tie affair in 1991.

*Lou with Mary Lou Whitney at a College of Saint Rose fund-
raiser at the Saratoga race track in 1991.*

*The Lake House, which has been in Linda Vaccaro's family for
generations, is located on Fourth Lake, part of the Fulton Chain of
Lakes in the Adirondacks, near Old Forge, New York.*

Chapter 14
Self-Study

Growing up with the kind of father I had, it was difficult for me to express myself emotionally. Our family life was tough and Papa always kept us busy. My parents were not demonstrative and so I learned to show my love by providing my family with the best I could afford. I needed to prove to myself that I could get ahead in my profession and provide for my growing family.

Jean was such a great mother; she bore the responsibility for raising the kids, and she was there for them when I was out working, traveling and supporting our family.

Looking back, I now see that I was definitely not connected emotionally. I was always focused on the next thing I was going to do, the next paper I was going to write, the next book, the next conference. It was easy for me to do these things because Jean was a great mother and took care of all of the things that needed to be handled, including providing affection for our children.

In a sense, I was completely unaware. I was in a fog, just pushing ahead, and not seeing the landscape and the danger points that should have given me a clue.

When you are aware, you pick up signals and signs, you see obstacles that need to be overcome. I was blind to those signs and perhaps it is because of the upbringing I had with an authoritative father. As a child, if I had shown any emotion, it would have caused Papa to erupt and come down on me very hard psychologically. It was easier to keep emotions hidden. I learned to be adept and expert at interacting with people on a non-emotional level. I became expert at suppressing my feelings.

Consequently, I became an expert at observing, listening, watching, and analyzing rather than connecting emotionally. That led me to eventually become an expert theorizer. I loved developing theory and strategies because these were not connected to emotion. It helped me in my work, in the practice of my duties as a college administrator. I learned a lot by listening, observing and emulating others. Father John Raynor was a superb theorizer. He was the guy I wanted to become because he was so successful and such an astute practitioner of educational theory and practice.

It comes as a surprise to people that I didn't grow up in a typical warm, loving Italian family. But, my parents didn't emotionally connect with me. There was never an embrace or a hug from my parents and only a few handshakes with Papa. As I grew older and had kids and became a husband and father, there were few of those initiated by me because I simply didn't know how.

I wish I had read Jean Vanier's book, "Becoming Human," before I actually did many years later. His central thesis is, "We learn to become human by connecting to people through our hearts and by knowing God through them." For me, another lesson learned—but somewhat late in life.

My inability to emotionally connect was one of the things that caused Jean to observe that, yes, we were married and had children but that I was "distant emotionally." Looking back, I can't blame her—she was an outstanding mother and great homemaker. But, sadly, I was unable to meet her needs and often the emotional needs of our children

Today, I take full responsibility for whatever pain that resulted from my own inability to deal with my emotional side. I might have been a great educational theorist, but I was totally lacking about emotions. I'm happy to say Linda is a very emotional person and she connects so well with people emotionally that she has helped me get in touch with that side of me that has been suppressed for so many years. I've been blessed to have two outstanding women as partners in my life. Linda holds my feet to the fire when it comes to emotional relationships with my children and I hope they can see that I love them beyond anything I can imagine.

Linda and I enjoy a unique and loving relationship. She has forced me to "emote and express myself" for wont of a better description. When she has listened to my talks and lectures, she has always told me I needed to be more emotional in my delivery. It's part of being fully human. And I'm working on repairing some of those damaged relationships that have faltered over the years because I was unable to show my feelings.

A great benefit of one's journey through life is the various lessons one learns along the way—some planned, but mostly wisdom acquired through living.

A typical Chinese banquet following completion of MBA Course at USTC.

Lou with two Chinese students and two campus Hotel Workers at USTC.

Louis C. Vaccaro

The Vaccaro Clan and friends celebrate at a family wedding.

*Linda and Lou Vaccaro share a swing at the Window
of the World Park in China, 2004.*

116

Afterword

Not for the first time, Lou Vaccaro has given me a challenging assignment: write an afterword to a biography about the man I have known for nearly 50 years. That task gave me cause to reflect on the many ways in which his life and mine have intertwined over the five decades. After reading a synopsis of *Around the Corner: From Shoeshine Boy to College President*, I recalled two instances not included in the biography, but that help illustrate several of Lou's attributes and were significant in my life.

During a very wet summer week a few years ago, my wife, Jane, and I called on the Vaccaros at their vacation home in the Adirondack Mountains. Lou and Linda spend their summers in this cozy cottage on Fourth Lake, a pleasant retreat that has been in her family for decades. In one of our far-ranging discussions during the visit, Lou encouraged me to consider teaching in China. He had made the same recommendation multiple times in his role as an educational consultant to China. Circumstances had kept me from saying "Yes" in previous years, but this time, after discussing it with Jane, I decided it was time to accept the opportunity.

Lou's continued prodding demonstrates several of his dominant characteristics: his desire to help others in their professional pursuits, his commitment to educational exchange between China and the United States, and his tenacity. Twenty-five years of hearing Lou's advice that teaching in China would be "a life-changing experience" finally had its desired effect. A few weeks after our visit with Lou and Linda, Jane and I armed ourselves with passports and visas and headed for Dalian, China, where I taught English at Dongbei University of Finance and Economics. Lou was right. My life was changed and shaped by my year in that fascinating culture and unique teaching environment.

The other instance had happened many years before. When he was named president of Colby-Sawyer College in the spring of 1972, he asked me to apply for the position of academic dean. I was honored to be asked and quickly accepted the invitation to visit the college for an interview. I was doubly honored when I was appointed Dean of the College. My experience in China 34 years later was an echo of my nine years at Colby: life-changing and life-shaping.

Lou and I met at Michigan State University in 1962. He was finishing his doctoral degree, and I was starting work toward a master's degree in English. We were close in age, we each had four daughters, and we lived two doors apart in married housing. As much as we enjoyed each other, socially and professionally, neither of us could have imagined what lay ahead in our careers that consistently criss-crossed. Lou, guided by the hand of God, moved me in directions I otherwise would have missed. His friendship has a magical quality that I noted not long after our first meeting. In March 1964 Lou and his family came from Milwaukee to visit me and my family in East Lansing, where I was in the final stage of completing my master's degree requirements. After they left, I wrote in my journal: "Vaccaros have come and gone. It seems as if we only got glimpses of them, from time to time. Lou exudes a warmth, a friendship, that I am compelled to embrace. It is not that he is like me, but more that we are not alike, yet he accepts me and I embrace him. He seems to say, 'Come, I like you and I take you without question, without doubt, without hypocrisy.' Lou is outward going and responds to everyone this way. Friendship with Lou is not earned or deserved, it simply is there." That sentiment, expressed so long ago, is just as fitting today, as his biography so aptly illustrates. *Around the Corner: From Shoeshine Boy to College President* is a substantive testimony to the man I have known. The man in the book and the man in my life are one. Congratulations, Lou, for leading an exemplary life, filled with love for God and family. Thanks also for lending a helping hand to hundreds of students and friends throughout your long and remarkable career.

Wallace K. Ewing, Ph.D.

Epilogue

This autobiography, as told to Renee Collins, was undertaken primarily for the benefit of my children, grandchildren and siblings. Whether or not it appeals to others will depend on how they view this story.

Will it appeal to others who have no relationship to me? Are there lessons within this story that can be useful to others? These are questions only a reader can answer.

Though this story is true—as I recall it following a long life—it is not a verbatim account of my life, nor is it a complete account.

Two years ago, when I spoke with Renee about my desire to leave a record for the benefit of my family and friends, she graciously offered to help me put it together. Renee is a 1980 graduate of Siena Heights and a 1982 graduate of the University of Toledo. After spending nearly 20 years in the newspaper business as a writer and editor, she now teaches journalism at Adrian College. She has known the Vaccaro family for many years.

I am indebted to Renee and I am also indebted to many others without whose help and advice this book would never have been born. Among the many friends and colleagues I must single out especially: Wally

Ewing, Jerry Gill, Paul Grondahl, and dozens of former students—primarily from China and Brazil. Of course, a special debt is owed to my children, all of whom provided memories and admonitions during a long life and who sacrificed much during their growing up years so that I might take advantage of opportunities offered along the way. Special appreciation goes to my former spouse and my current wife.

Did I always make the right choices along the way? Not by a long shot! One could say I certainly should have done much better.

In this story, I have tried to pay homage to my grandparents, my mother, my father and countless uncles, aunts and cousins. It was the strong guidance and counsel of these loved ones—coupled with the professional and personal friendships from teachers, mentors and colleagues throughout my professional and academic career that allowed me to benefit so greatly. I will always be forever grateful.

As I write this epilogue, I am planning what may be my final academic assignment as a senior Fulbright specialist in Indonesia. Interestingly, my first academic assignment following graduation from Michigan State University was with the Jesuits at Marquette University in Milwaukee, Wisconsin. My final academic assignment will be with the Jesuits at Sanata Dharma University in Yogyakarta, Indonesia. So I guess you could say I've come full circle.

I have often said that one's life does not always follow one's plan, but consists of our striving to discover God's plan for our life. Life, indeed, is a journey—one fraught with ups and downs, challenges and opportunities. Our task is to seek and discover God's plan and to follow it as best we can.

I have not always succeeded in this quest, due primarily to the all too human weaknesses of pride and vanity. Along the way, I have attempted to treat each person in my life with dignity and respect. But, indeed, the spirit is willing but the flesh is weak. What is important is staying true to the Jesuit motto: *ad majorem dei glorium*, "All for the greater glory of God."

Lou in January 2011 in Indonesia with his Muslim colleague from the Islamic University in Yogyakarta, Professor Zain Ruduain, the professor's mother-in-law (in head scarf), the professor's wife, and his newborn baby. Lou had just concluded a walk with the professor through his village.

Lou with Father Paulus Wiryono Priyotamtama, S.J., Rector of Sanata Dharma University in Indonesia. Father Paul was Lou's host in January 2011 when he visited the island nation on a Fulbright scholarship.

Biography

Louis C. Vaccaro has served as president of several colleges, including two interim assignments at Trinity College of Vermont and Georgian Court University in Lakewood, N.J. He has served as president of The College of Saint Rose in Albany, N.Y., Siena Heights University in Adrian, Michigan; and Colby-Sawyer College in New London, New Hampshire.

Early in his career, he served in a variety of administrative and faculty positions at St. Mary's College, Notre Dame, Indiana; California State University-Northridge; Marquette University, Milwaukee, Wisconsin; and the University of Portland, Oregon. During the 1966-67 academic year, he completed post-doctoral studies in organizational sociology at The University of Oregon.

Dr. Vaccaro earned his bachelor of arts degree in economics and social sciences as well as a master of arts degree from the University of Southern California, and completed a second master's degree at California State University in Northridge. He finished his doctorate in higher education and sociology at Michigan State University.

The author and editor of 7 books and more than 100 articles and book reviews, Dr. Vaccaro's most recent focus has been in the fields of higher education and organizational change. He was awarded a Kellogg Fellowship by Michigan State University and a grant from the Exxon Foundation for research in strategic planning. He also has served as a senior Fulbright specialist in Honduras and Indonesia.

In the mid-1970s, Dr. Vaccaro began a 10-year, part-time assignment as a lecturer and consultant in Brazil, first under the auspices of the Fletcher School of Law and Diplomacy of Tufts University and later with the Latin American Studies Center of Michigan State University.

In 1978, Dr. Vaccaro started lecturing and consulting part-time in China. Since then, he has traveled to China on 34 occasions, arranging several bilateral student and faculty exchange programs with leading Chinese colleges and universities.

Throughout his career, he has been a frequent contributor to higher education organizations in various parts of the United States. During the 1975-76 academic year, he served as chair of the New Hampshire Post-Secondary Education Commission. He later served as chair of the Independent College Fund of New York.

Dr. Vaccaro has received several awards and honors, including honorary degrees from Vermont College of Norwich University, St. Martin's College, Olympia, Washington; and The College of Saint Rose in Albany. In 1996, he was named Honorary Distinguished Professor of Dalian Normal University in China, and has served as Distinguished Visiting Professor at USTC in Hefei and Shanghai. In 2001 he was named Honorary President of Aurora College in Shanghai, China. He also was honored by the University of Albany, SUNY, as the Academic Citizen Laureate in 1995, and in 1989 received the Golden Lion Award from the Sons of Italy, Intangible Lodge, Albany.

A native Californian, Dr. Vaccaro and his wife, Linda, split their time between Las Vegas, Nevada and Old Forge, New York.